THE
BEARDSTOWN LADIES'
COMMON-SENSE
INVESTMENT
GUIDE

THE
BEARDSTOWN LADIES'
COMMON-SENSE
INVESTMENT
GUIDE

How We Beat the
Stock Market—And
How You Can Too

by The Beardstown Ladies
Investment Club
with Leslie Whitaker

A Seth Godin Production

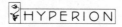

New York

NOTE: Investment clubs commonly compute their annual "return" by calculating the increase in their total club balance over a period of time. Since this increase includes the dues that the members pay regularly, this "return" may be different from the return that might be calculated for a mutual fund or a bank. Since the regular contributions are an important part of the club philosophy, the Ladies' returns described in this book are based on this common calculation.

Charts and text on pages 48, 49, 92, 93, 95, 102, 114, 132, and 137 reproduced with the kind permission of NAIC and the Investors Manual: P.O. Box 220, Royal Oak, Michigan 48068.

Value Line report on Rubbermaid copyright 1994 by Value Line Publishing, Inc. Reprinted by permission; all rights reserved.

Library of Congress Cataloging-in-Publication Data
Beardstown Ladies Investment Club.
    The Beardstown Ladies' common sense investment guide: how we beat the stock market—and how you can too / by the Beardstown Ladies Investment Club with Leslie Whitaker. — 1st ed.
        p. cm.
    ISBN 0-7868-6043-X
    1. Investments—United States—Handbooks, manuals, etc. 2. Women in business—United States—Handbooks, manuals, etc. 3. Women—United States—Finance, Personal—Handbooks, manuals, etc. 4. Saving and thrift—United States—Handbooks, manuals, etc. I. Whitaker, Leslie. II. Title. III. Title: Common sense investment guide.
HG4527.B37 1994
332.63′22—dc20   94-19423
                                                                    CIP

Illustrations by Mary A. Wirth

10   9

Dedication

We dedicate this book to Margaret H. Greenman, Charter Member and First Senior Partner. "Aunt" Margaret's dedication to our investment education was a motivating force in the success that we have known. Her death on April 6, 1987, came just as we were beginning to enjoy our first real profits, which she helped to make happen!

—The Beardstown Ladies

Acknowledgments

From the Beardstown Ladies:

Homer G. Rieken, Broker, A. G. Edwards & Sons, Inc., Springfield, Illinois

    Homer was instrumental in helping to organize the Investment Club and gave enthusiastic encouragement through the years

First State Bank of Beardstown, Illinois

First National Bank of Beardstown, Illinois

The Havana National Bank of Havana, Illinois

First Evangelical Lutheran Church of Beardstown, Illinois, provided a place for our monthly meetings

From the writer:

Thanks to Bernie Whitaker, Orin Whitaker, Elizabeth Austin, Jim Rank, and David Kliff, Certified Financial Planner and Registered Investment Advisor.

Keith Colter and Carolyn Patterson at Central Picture are the visionaries who first realized that the Ladies' story needed to be told. This book would not have existed without their input and enthusiasm. Thanks also to Lisa DiMona, Megan O'Connor, Julie Maner, Karen Watts, Carol Markowitz, Jen Gniady, and Lucy Wood. Special thanks to Bob Miller and to Mary Ann Naples, our extraordinary editor at Hyperion.

With love to Michael and Benjamin.

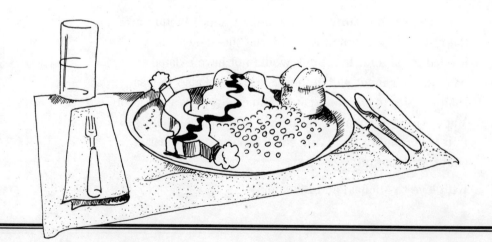

Contents

Contents

Introduction

The Beardstown Ladies vs. the Experts

I f you wanted to find the greatest investment minds of our generation, you might start your search in New York; or Zurich; or Tokyo. But after meeting with self-important MBAs in split skirts or three-piece suits, you might be wise enough to hop on a plane and fly to Chicago. There, you'd rent a car and drive for several hours (though it seems like more) through cornfields and more cornfields, to Springfield, the sleepy capital of Illinois. Having fortified yourself with a tuna sandwich on white bread, spend another hour in the car and you'll arrive in Beardstown, Illinois.

For the past 10 years, 16 women who belong to an investment club in Beardstown have outpaced and outclassed most other devotees of the stock market. Named an "All-Star Club" for six years in a row by the National Association of Investors Corporation (NAIC), a not-for-profit organization that provides investor education and tracks the performance of investment clubs, the Beardstown Business and Professional Women's Investment Club (their formal name) has achieved more recognition than the other 11,000 investment clubs across the country. Their hand-picked portfolio of fewer than 20 stocks has earned an average annual return of 23.4%—twice that of the Standard & Poor's 500 and more than most professional money managers. In 1991, the club's best year to date, its return on stocks listed on the New York Stock Exchange was a staggering 59.5%.

Although the Beardstown Ladies, as they've come to be known, won't take your money, if you'd given them $100 in 1983, you'd have more than $1,000 today.

How do they do it?

By doing their *own* homework, rather than relying on the advice of investment gurus, and by rigorously observing some straightforward investing principles—like investing regularly, regardless of the ups and downs of the market.

Each member of the club contributes just $25 every month to invest. Yet, through educated investing, the club's portfolio has grown to more than $80,000. The Ladies, many of whom had no investments when they started, also apply what they learn in the club to managing and building their personal portfolios, which include CDs, bonds, Treasury notes, real estate, and mutual funds as well as stocks.

Legendary mutual fund manager Peter Lynch maintains that ordinary people have the edge over the high-flying experts on Wall Street when it comes to picking stocks. "Twenty years in this business convinces me that any normal person using the customary three percent of the brain can pick stocks just as well, if not better, than the average Wall Street expert," he wrote in *One Up on Wall Street*, his best-selling book. "If you stay half-alert, you can pick the spectacular performers right from your place of business or out of the neighborhood shopping mall, and long before Wall Street discovers them."

The Beardstown Ladies have proven Lynch right. For the past decade, they have used what they observed in their small farming community (pop. 6,000) on the banks of the Illinois River to guide their investment decisions. They have also studied NAIC's educational materials and adapted them for their own use. The results have been a portfolio of profits and a book's worth of lessons on successful investing.

Like most individual investors, the Beardstown Ladies are ordinary people. Most have lived all of their lives in a small town. They range in age from 41 to 87. Most are retired and several are widows. Many know how to farm, having been raised on one or worked on one as an adult. In total, they have raised 30 children and loved 40 grandchildren and seven great-grandchildren.

Several worked outside the home long before there was a big fuss about it. Partners include a school principal, a secretary, a retired bank officer, the co-owner of a hog farm, a florist and gift shop owner, a real estate broker, and a retired medical technologist. Beardstown's local banks have only three women on their boards of directors; all three are club members.

The Ladies have helped each other advance in their careers when they could, yet never thought of it as mentoring or networking, more as friends helping friends. They are religious people, active in churches and volunteer organizations around town. The investment club is only one of many meetings they attend every month.

So when it came to investing, most of them knew very little when they started their club. What brought them together, quite simply, was a desire to learn how to better manage their personal assets.

Today, the Beardstown Ladies are celebrities. They have

appeared as guests on numerous television shows, including *CBS This Morning* and *John and Leeza*. They have been the subject of articles in scores of publications, including *U.S. News & World Report, Money, Working Woman, Modern Maturity*, and *Kiplinger's Personal Finance*. They even appear in an award-winning instructional video, "Cookin' Up Profits on Wall Street," which *Money* magazine called "the most entertaining" tape on the subject.

Several of the club's admirers—including a brokerage firm and the president of a watch company—have offered to pay generous sums for their investment advice. Others have asked the club to invest money for them. The Ladies could not accept those offers, even if they wanted to, because they are not licensed brokers. They graciously declined.

In fact, the club's first priority is to learn about the stock market and other investments. Members study educational materials, invite investment experts to speak at their meetings, and read the financial press regularly.

The club's second goal is enjoyment. They share meals, swap recipes, take trips together, and laugh when stocks they have chosen don't perform well. Many of the women have formed extremely close friendships over the years.

Their third goal is making a profit. The Ladies have written this book to share their homespun method for making profitable investments. It is for individuals who want to invest, either on their own, as a member of a club, or both. They explain how to get a club started, how to pick stocks, and how to avoid some of their early mistakes. With the benefit of the Ladies' experience on your side, learning how to invest should be fun and less intimidating than it ever was before. Remember, the Ladies started from scratch, too. Good luck, and, as the Ladies say, do your homework!

Who's Who in the Club

Ann Brewer, 60, secretary, charter member.

Ann Corley, 66, retired homemaker, member since 1985.

Doris Edwards, 72, elementary school principal, charter member.

Lillian Ellis, 77, retired dental assistant, charter member.

Sylvia Gaushell, 82, retired art teacher, member since 1991.

Shirley Gross, 77, retired medical technologist, charter member.

Margaret Houchins, 53, gift and flower shop owner, member since 1990.

Ruth Huston, 75, retired owner of a dry-cleaning business, charter member.

Carnell Korsmeyer, 67, hog farm owner, member National Pork Board, charter member.

Helen Kramer, 78, retired bank officer, charter member.

Hazel Lindahl, 87, retired school nurse, charter member.

Carol McCombs, 44, insurance agency employee, Elsie Scheer's daughter, new member.

Elsie Scheer, 76, retired farmer and teacher's aide, charter member.

Betty Sinnock, 62, bank trust officer, charter member.

Maxine Thomas, 73, retired bank teller, charter member.

Buffy Tillitt-Pratt, 41, real estate broker, member since 1987.

A Few Words About Beardstown

There are not many places like Beardstown, Illinois. It's not only safe to leave your car unlocked, but you can leave your keys in the ignition. Not everyone knows one another in this town of 6,000, but just about. And if you don't know enough about your neighbors, you can find out more by looking them up in the telephone book, which lists their occupation and the years that their children were born.

Located 225 miles southwest of Chicago on the banks of the Illinois River, Beardstown's gently rolling hills were settled in 1819 by Thomas Beard, who traveled to Illinois from Ohio on horseback. Beard built a log cabin at the river's edge and began trading with the Indians. A two-story brick building he erected later was used as a store and an inn, where Abe Lincoln stayed as a young lawyer when he came to Beardstown from Springfield.

One of Lincoln's most famous cases, known as the Almanac Trial, was tried in the historic Cass County Courthouse, which stands on Beardstown's City Square. Lincoln successfully defended Duff Armstrong, the son of a friend, on a charge of murdering a man during a fight after a revival camp meeting. The key witness against Armstrong claimed that he had seen the fight by the light of the high moon, at about 10:00 or 11:00 P.M. Lincoln displayed an 1857 almanac showing that on August 29, the moon set a little before midnight, and Duff was acquitted. Still in use today, the courthouse remains as it was when Lincoln practiced there.

Across from the courthouse, Lincoln and Stephen Douglas announced their campaigns for a seat in the United States Senate. Though Lincoln lost that race, the debates during the campaign did much to further his political reputation.

During its early years, Beardstown was larger than Chicago; a flourishing port, it supplied interior towns with grain, hogs and general provisions. Well known for its stockyards and slaughterhouses, Beardstown was often called "Porkopolis." Fishing was also an important industry. Hauls included black bass, German carp, buffalo, crappie, eel, catfish, frogs, and turtles. Once famous for its marina, Beardstown was a boat stop for river travelers.

The natural ice industry was a thriving business that employed hundreds of men and boys until the first artificial ice plant was installed in 1907. They harvested ice out on the bay when weather conditions made it possible. Large blocks of ice were packed in sawdust and stored in four large ice houses for local delivery the following summer.

The first train ran out of Beardstown in the summer of 1870. The citizens had to raise money for a bond of $150,000, which was paid to the railroad, to secure itself a stop. The St. Louis, Rock Island, and Chicago Division of the Chicago,

Burlington and Quincy Railroad was Beardstown's main industry for nearly 50 years. Shop whistles signaling the end of a shift could be heard all over town.

Today, Beardstown is home to farmers, small businessmen and women, employees of local utilities, and one of the largest hog slaughterers in the world. Corn, soybeans, and watermelons are among the largest crops. As Chicago has grown, Beardstown has stayed small. But the people are not small-minded. To the contrary, if the 16 women of the Beardstown Business and Professional Women's Investment Club are any measure, they're industrious people with at least one interesting story to tell.

STARTING
A CLUB

1. Investment Clubs: A Low-Cost Way to Learn

Consider the case of the Mutual Investment Club of Detroit, one of the oldest investment clubs in the country. Members who joined the club at the outset in 1941, and contributed a total of $291,045 over the next 30 years, reaped an investment worth many times that amount. They withdrew $1,310,411 during that period, and still the liquidating value of their investment in 1992 was $2,109,917.

When the Beardstown Business and Professional Women's Investment Club was established in 1983, it became part of a much larger community of individuals across the country who have been forming clubs for many decades with the purpose of investing in and studying the stock market.

Of course, joining a club does not guarantee success. The clubs that have matched our return record—an average annual return of 23.4% for a 10-year period—have been few and far between. The performance of the thousands of clubs currently in existence varies widely, depending largely on the members' commitment to serious investing. On average, however, their yearly returns are close to 15%, which beats the Dow Jones Industrial Average's average annual gain of 10%. In fact, the average portfolio of clubs tracked by the National Association of Investors Corp. earned more than S&P's 500 Index in all but seven of the last 29 years. The average investment club is 11 years old and has a portfolio worth $100,000.

The advantages of joining a club are many. By investing as a part of a group rather than individually, members share the burden of managing their investment with others. Because clubs divide up the work of studying stocks among members, you can learn about many more companies and industries in a single club meeting that you could in hours of investigation on your own. Clubs can serve as a bellwether for your personal portfolio. Membership can last a lifetime and can lead to close friendships, an advantage that we have certainly enjoyed.

Don't rule out joining a club if you are new to investing, or if you are an old hand. We have found that clubs benefit from both types of investors and the groups that combine both work best. Some clubs restrict their membership to men or to women, while others admit both sexes. You should affiliate with one where you feel most comfortable. We do not recommend any membership model, though we do note with pride that all-female clubs tracked by NAIC have outperformed all-male clubs, with a lifetime earning rate of 10.5% vs. 9.7%.

The first known investment club was set up in Texas in 1898. Investment clubs began operating in Europe in about

1900. The concept was revived in the United States by servicemen who had fought in Europe during World War II. With money coming in and most of their expenses paid, some United States soldiers began to pool money for investment purposes while they were still enlisted. Once the war was over, the investment club movement took off in the United States. The movement hit a peak in 1970, when 14,101 clubs were affiliated with NAIC, the not-for-profit organization that assists individual investors and clubs. Since NAIC was founded in 1951 by financial analyst George A. Nicholson and his friends Frederick C. Russell and Thomas E. O'Hara, the organization has developed educational materials and programs that help investors evaluate stocks and manage portfolios. NAIC's regional councils offer in-depth educational seminars on such topics as evaluating and selecting stocks for local clubs.

Membership has risen steadily since 1980, when NAIC's roster hit a low point of 3,100 clubs. Today, NAIC has more than 12,000 club, 49,532 individual, and 208 corporate members, with enthusiasts ranging in age from teenagers to octogenarians. Investment club associations have also been established in 17 foreign countries.

Most American clubs model themselves after the Mutual Investment Club of Detroit, one of the first modern investment clubs. Typical club goals are:

1. Invest every month;
2. reinvest all dividends;
3. buy growth companies; and
4. diversify.

Dues average $35 a month, an amount that most people can afford to risk. Being in a club establishes a pattern of investing regularly, which averages out costs over the ups and downs of the market: though investors can afford fewer

A Personal Testimonial

Betty Sinnock spoke about the investment club at Beardstown's chapter of Business and Professional Women (BPW). I had heard the term "investment club" before, but I always thought it was for rich people. I decided to join soon after I heard Betty's talk.

I have learned a great deal because I grew up in a family that was not wealthy by any means. We lived practically from paycheck to paycheck. Even though my mom and dad were able to put a few dollars in a savings account, they were never introduced to investments, the stock market, Wall Street, any of that. But in the back of my mind I was always interested in Wall Street and buying stocks.

To get the most out of the many educational resources available to investors today, you may have to draw on your reserve of patience and persistence, however. The first time I attended an NAIC Stock Selection Guide seminar, for instance, everything was Greek to me. I grasped maybe 10%, and that's stretching it. It was kind of overwhelming. The other ladies, of course, they have been in it for years and years and they were absorbing it all, and I wondered "Will I ever grasp this?"

We have done quite a bit of education in our club. It's not that I understand all the terminology, but terms like "p/e ratios" and "upside-down ratios" are becoming clearer. A year later I attended the same seminar, and I would say I grasped 90%.

My knowledge is increasing as I stay in the club. When I hear a reference to the Dow Jones on the television, I stop what I'm doing and listen. It's an exciting new adventure and you really get caught up in it.

—*Margaret Houchins*

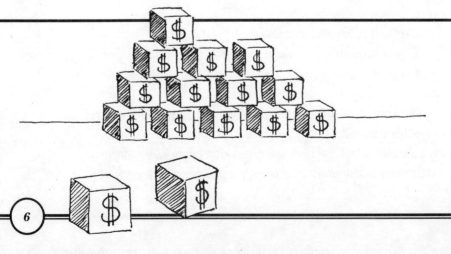

shares when prices are lofty, they benefit when prices are depressed because they can purchase more shares. Ideally, members should not draw on their investment for many years.

If you are interested in joining a club but there is not one already established in your area, NAIC can provide many of the materials you need to start one up. A club requires finding 10 to 20 members who can function well as a team and who share the same long-term investment philosophy. If some members are committed to long-term investing and others want to buy and sell based on the short-term fluctuations of the market, a club will quickly dissolve.

NAIC officials have found that 40% of the clubs that form break up within two years, usually because some members expect, wrongly, that an investment club is a scheme to get rich quick. In fact, they are a way to steadily increase your investment in and understanding of the stock market. John D. Rockefeller offers some useful wisdom: "The man who starts out simply with the idea of getting rich won't succeed; you must have a larger ambition."

Clubs can of course operate independently of NAIC, but we have found that affiliating with that organization affords members many advantages. (A club can join for $35 a year, plus $11 for each member.) Each partner receives a subscription to NAIC's monthly magazine, *Better Investing*, which is full of educational information and investment tips, such as the Stock Selection Guide, a step-by-step tool for evaluating stocks before investing. Other useful materials include the *Investors Manual*, which outlines NAIC's program for managing a portfolio, *Investors Information Reports*, financial information on more than 100 companies, and step-by-step instructions on how to use the Stock Comparison Guide, a form that helps investors compare stocks.

A "Low-Cost Investment Plan" is also open to NAIC members. This plan allows individuals to begin investing through

NAIC by purchasing just one share of stock for the price of the stock plus a minimal fee. You can choose from among 120 companies that participate in the plan, including AT&T, McDonald's, Ryder Systems, and Kellogg's. After you buy one share, your account will be managed by the company's dividend reinvestment plan and you can add to your holdings with regular contributions, set at whatever level you can afford. It's an easy, low-cost way to get a personal or club portfolio started. Many of our partners invest on their own this way.

2. Why We Started The Beardstown Club: Our Story

Aunt Margaret was 80 years old when Betty moved her from southern Illinois to Beardstown so she could be close at hand. Margaret didn't have any children, so Betty looked after her.

Soon after Aunt Margaret moved to Beardstown, Betty encouraged her to join the local chapter of Business and Professional Women (BPW), a national organization that promotes equity and economic self-sufficiency for working women. Betty was program chairman at the time and many of the women in town had been members for years. Betty thought joining "BP doubla-ya"—as we pronounce it here in central Illinois—would be a good way for Aunt Margaret,

Shirley's Search for a Broker

In the 1970s, I wanted to invest in utility stocks, but I had a heck of a time finding a broker who would accept me as a client. At the time, brokerage houses were not particularly friendly places for women. There were few female brokers, and women, particularly older ones, were not considered desirable clients.

There was a broker from Jacksonville, Illinois, who came over one afternoon a week to Beardstown. I left a note for him to either call or come by and see me because I wanted to buy some utility stocks. He didn't come. The next week I went down and asked the secretary what happened. She said, "I gave him your note." So I told her, "When he comes in today, find out why he didn't come and I'll still be home this afternoon to hear from him." I still didn't hear from him, so I called her. The answer was simple: he didn't want to be bothered with retired women.

Shortly after that, our church was renting out our dining room to a brokerage firm from Quincy. A young broker was coming over to look for business in Beardstown, so I signed up for his seminar.

It was a mixed group, both men and women. Every time there was a chance to ask a question, I had my hand up. He never once called on me; always the men. I was very conscious of the fact that only the men were talking and the rest of us were sitting there like we didn't know anything.

When the evening was over, I pinned him down and said there were several stocks I was interested in, what did he think of them? He didn't follow them, but said he would check into it and give me a call.

The next morning he called and said, "Those are good stocks. But I talked to my boss and he said that we didn't want you as a client because you are an artist." (He had seen me showing some of my drawings to the church's deaconess.) My primary income is from farming, so you take it from there. Should I be turned down as a client because I can draw?

Later, my brother, who had been a member of an investment club at one time, recommended Homer Rieken in A. G. Edward's Springfield office. Rieken had been his club's broker.

I called Homer and made an appointment; I even found a dress and got all gussied up. And to top it off, I went down to the bank and had the bank president write me a letter of credit. I wasn't going to get turned down a third time. There is absolutely no reason why women cannot buy stocks and I was determined to find a broker who would take me seriously.

I went over to see Homer. He looked at the letter of credit, tossed it across his desk, and said, "You didn't need to do that. In the first place, if you buy a stock and you don't pay for it, you don't get it. There is no reason why a broker should turn down anybody if he is looking for business. I welcome you as a client." We have been together ever since.

Not dismayed by my artistic ability, Homer later bought one of my paintings at a fund-raiser for the Beardstown Restoration Society and it still hangs in his office. When we formed the investment club, I already knew Homer and suggested we use him as our broker. He not only encouraged us, he came over for our first two or three meetings and told us how to get organized. It was Homer who helped us do it.

—*Shirley Gross*

who had been a school administrator and an author, to meet new friends.

In 1980, BPW's national office in Washington, D.C., proposed that local chapters form investment clubs so members could learn how to manage their financial assets. The rationale was that many of the members were single, some were divorced, and most of the married ones would probably face widowhood at one time or another.

Betty was a customer service representative at Beardstown's First National Bank at the time, but she knew nothing about the stock market. "I thought the only meaning of portfolio was 'briefcase,' " she laughs. "Seeing people with real wealth coming in with their dividend checks when I worked as a teller and knowing that they had something besides a bank investment, I just simply wanted to learn."

Shirley Gross, already a serious investor at the time, was also enthusiastic. When Shirley had first tried to invest in stocks in the mid-1970s, she had a difficult time finding a broker who would take her on as a client (see sidebar, p. 10). She endorsed any program that would ease the way for other women who wanted to invest.

About 36 women, members of the Beardstown BPW and others from the community, joined the investment club, which organized monthly programs on all types of investments, including municipal, convertible, and corporate bonds, Treasuries, money market funds, and certificates of deposit (CDs). At the same time, members studied stocks and began to invest in the market. Club members contributed anywhere from $5 to $30 a month for investment purposes.

When Aunt Margaret first came to Beardstown, she had put all of her money in bank CDs. "In our family there were stories about how so-and-so's father had lost two or three fortunes in the market and the market was just a no-no. It was taboo. You didn't even discuss it," Betty explains. Along with Betty, Margaret joined the local BPW investment club.

Margaret became extremely interested in investing in the market.

Betty was a member of the first Stock Study Committee and recalls going to Shirley's house to hunt for potential investments because Shirley subscribed to *The Wall Street Journal* and *Value Line*.

"She told us what she thought we needed to know about *Value Line* and how to look up a stock's price in the *Journal* and then went off into the other room and left us. This was good because we were able to make our own choices. We saw that *Value Line* rated stocks from one to five on safety and timeliness and we didn't want the lowest ones. Sometimes a committee member would suggest a stock that a friend had recommended to them. We were kind of haphazard at first."

During the three years the first group was together, their investments included A. G. Edwards, American Home Products, Dow Jones, Kellogg's, and PepsiCo. After three years, as per its charter, the group disbanded.

Aunt Margaret was heartbroken. "She felt like her world had tumbled upside down," says Betty. So Betty telephoned the most active club members and proposed reorganizing. A meeting date was set and 12 of the original members and four others showed up. On November 3, 1983, in the First National Bank's boardroom, the Beardstown Business and Professional Women's Investment Club was reestablished.

Charter members signed a partnership agreement and settled on three goals: (1) education; (2) enjoyment; and (3) financial enrichment—in that order. Following the counsel of NAIC and of Homer Reiken, Shirley's broker at A. G. Edwards, we decided to restrict our investments to growth stocks and hold them on a long-term basis. Our financial goal was a 14.7% return per year, which would double our money every five years.

Aunt Margaret continued to be an active participant in

the new club and began to invest on her own. One time, for instance, the group discussed investing in Kellogg's, but decided against it. Impressed by the company, Margaret called Homer, who had agreed to become the club's broker, and told him she wanted to personally invest in 300 shares of the cereal maker. The stock subsequently climbed, and with the money she made in 16 months she bought a car, a new 1985 Chrysler New Yorker. She had nearly tripled her investment.

By the time she died in 1987 at age 85, Aunt Margaret's estate was worth $470,000, almost double the amount she had brought to Beardstown. The club's first deceased member, she is greatly missed.

3. Setting Up a Successful Investment Club: The Fundamentals

Thousands of investment clubs around the country share a commitment to supporting the business world through their investments. But there are many variations on the structure and operating rules of those clubs. In size, they range from as few as three members to more than 50. Some specify club dues, others allow members to vary their contributions every month. And some are more serious about the business of investing, while others spend most of their time socializing.

Despite their good intentions, roughly 40% of all new investment clubs shut down after two years. We've been going strong for 10 years. Based on our experience, here's what you need to know to establish a long-lasting, effective club:

Setting Goals

Setting goals at the outset is critical to establishing a durable club. NAIC officials have found that most investment clubs that disband after two years are victims of a get-rich-quick mentality among some members. The Beardstown Ladies' three goals, in contrast, put making money last. Our goals can be expressed as the Three E's:

(1) Education;

(2) enjoyment; and

(3) financial enrichment.

The Importance of Education

Whatever its other goals, an investment club's primary purpose should be to serve as a forum in which its members can learn about the stock market. Partners should learn something new at every meeting. If your club's members have varying degrees of experience in the stock market, pair more seasoned investors with those who are just starting out in committees so they can work together.

Members should also be encouraged to attend educational seminars, especially those sponsored by NAIC's regional organizations. Usually held on weekends, these seminars provide intensive introductions to investing and can be pleasurable field trips to take with fellow investors.

The Importance of Enjoyment

Enjoyment is critical to a successful club. While it is always fun to make money, you've got to keep interest and spirits high when the market lags, because investing during a down market reaps great rewards when it rebounds.

Food always brings people out. Try holding meetings at local restaurants or having potluck dinners at a member's house before a meeting (see Chapter 20 if you are short on recipes). Touring your broker's office or taking trips together to sites of financial interest—a local company in which you have invested or the nearest stock exchange—is also fun as well as educational.

Is 16 Members a Magic Number?

Definitely not. Most clubs have somewhere between 10 and 25 members. We settled on 16 members simply because that is the number of women who showed up at our organizing meeting. You need enough members to follow a diverse range of stocks (each member tracks one or two stocks), but not too many for decision making. Part of the fun of a group is the lively discussions that come from mixing people with diverse experiences.

Search among your friends for members. You need a group that can work well as a team and that includes only members who are committed to doing the necessary preparation for each meeting, generally a few hours every month.

Once you settle on your own magic number, membership in the club should be fixed from the start, with new members admitted only upon the departure of an existing member. Our bylaws state that any new member must be acceptable to the entire group.

Some clubs admit members who are away for extended periods, to Florida vacation homes, for instance. They should be required to submit their dues in advance and are restricted from voting on club matters while they are away. If a partner is only going to miss one or two meetings, you may allow her to leave a proxy with another partner.

Partnership or Corporation?

Early on, you must determine the structure of your club. Investment clubs can be set up either as partnerships or corporations, but a partnership affords members more tax advantages. If it is set up as a corporation, an investment club's earnings are subject to two taxes: the club must pay corporate-level income tax on the corporation's earnings, and its members, considered shareholders of the corporation, must pay individual income tax on the distribution of corporate earnings as dividends. A partnership does not have to pay any taxes. Instead, each partner is responsible for reporting his or her share of the club's income on a personal tax return every year. When a partner withdraws from a club or when a club dissolves, he will only have to pay taxes on the income he has not already reported and paid taxes on.

Under current Treasury Department regulations, most clubs qualify for partnership status for tax purposes. But each club should consult with an attorney and an accountant to verify that status, based on its operating agreement, and determine if there are any state or local regulations that require yearly filings or fees. In Michigan, for example, clubs established as corporations have to file an annual report with the state and pay a franchise fee. At least three states— Illinois, Wisconsin, and New Mexico—consider investment club membership a security and impose filing requirements. (For more detail on setting up investment clubs as partnerships or corporations, consult NAIC's *Investors Manual*, pp. 13–19.)

Operating Agreement

Every group needs to draft an operating agreement that outlines its rules. This agreement must be acceptable to both members and legal authorities. During the drafting process, consult an attorney to make sure you are adhering to all federal, state, and local regulations that affect investment clubs.

The purpose of the club should be stated and limited to "invest the assets of the partnership in stocks for the education and benefit of the partners" or something similar. This wording limits the authority of any single partner, a safeguard against fraud. (See Beardstown Ladies' Partnership Agreement, p. 24.)

Liability

The members of a club can be held liable for the wrongful action of a club's agents in the course of club business. Because a club's only business is buying and selling securities, however, it is fairly easy to keep track of its transactions. The treasurer should circulate the broker's statement to all members at each meeting, to verify that last month's dues were deposited, no unauthorized disbursements were made, and securities that were ordered were purchased. To date, the NAIC has uncovered no litigation stemming from investment club membership.

Club Name

Choose a name that clearly states the purpose of the club. The Beardstown Professional and Business Women's Investment Club is probably more cumbersome than a club's name needs to be. The Investment Club of Peoria, in contrast, is straightforward and simple.

How Many Officers?

Four officers make for a well-run club—a senior partner, a junior partner, a recording partner, and a financial partner.

The *senior partner* oversees the activities of the club.

She sets the meeting time and place, appoints committees, and conducts monthly meetings.

The *junior partner* assumes the senior partner's duties, if the senior partner is unavailable. She is also responsible for providing or organizing the educational content of the meetings, usually a 10- to 15-minute presentation. Popular presentations include going through a Stock Selection Guide with the group, reading a column from a financial columnist, or listening to a talk on "dollar cost averaging" or some other investment technique by a local broker.

The *recording partner* is responsible for taking the minutes of each meeting. She reads the minutes of the last meeting at the start of every session and makes corrections, if needed. The minutes are then approved by the group with a voice vote. The recording partner is also responsible for keeping all of the club's minutes.

The *financial partner* is central to the group. She maintains the club's financial records and places buy and sell orders with the club's broker. She receives all correspondence for the club, and also prepares a monthly statement of the club's receipts and disbursements and each member's interest in the club. In addition, she must prepare the annual tax information for each partner. The partnership does not file a tax return or pay taxes; instead, each partner must pay taxes on her share of the partnership's profits. (NAIC offers a computer program for club recordkeeping, which our financial partner, Betty Sinnock, has found to be a real time saver.)

Elect Officers Annually

We appoint a nominating committee. It is a good idea to rotate responsibilities among the group. However, if you find that one member is willing to be financial partner, which requires the most effort and knowledge, for several years, that can work well. Betty Sinnock has served as our financial partner for eight years.

Individual Responsibility

Each member should assume responsibility for tracking at least one of the club's investments. The financial partner, who will receive all correspondence from the corporations in which the club invests, should forward materials such as quarterly and annual reports to the member assigned to that specific stock. Other members who spot articles in the press about one of the club's investments should forward copies to the member following the stock.

At club meetings, each partner should make a brief presentation about her stock, noting stock price movement and important developments. If there are reasons for selling the stock, this is the time to open the discussion to the whole group. (For more information about selling your stock, see p. 128.)

Monthly Contribution

Some clubs allow members to contribute a different amount every month, which can be an accountant's nightmare. It is far simpler to keep track of each member's account if there is a fixed amount due at every meeting. We collect $25, which we refer to as our "tuition." The dollar amount is credited to each individual member's account.

In our club, new members are asked to pay a $100 initiation fee, which goes toward their NAIC membership and manual and their investment account. New members are offered the option of contributing money up to the amount in accounts opened earlier by charter members, currently $6,000. Partners' shares are tracked as investment credit units. (See NAIC's Unit Value System, p. 48.)

Voting

No matter what the value of a member's account, we feel she should have an equal vote. Clubs that give more votes to members with more money invested often develop power struggles between old and new members, with new members losing out. For buying and selling decisions, majority rules. In all other club business, a two-thirds majority is required to pass a motion. A quorum of two-thirds should be present for a vote.

Recordkeeping

The club should keep minutes of every meeting. These do not have to be elaborate and can be handwritten or typed. But they should include where the meeting was held, how many partners were present, the business of the meeting (including an update of the club's account), what stocks were reported on, and what buy and sell orders were agreed upon. (See sample minutes, p. 41.)

Investment Criteria

Although you will learn more about our investment methods later in the book, we have briefly outlined our basic guidelines here. We believe that the key to successful investing is time, not timing. You need a group that is willing to study stocks as it decides which ones to buy, and that will hold on to those stocks for the long term. Of course, there are always exceptions. But selling decisions should be based on a set of pre-established criteria, never on a whim. (see When to Sell, p. 127).

Price Range

You might want to agree upon a price range for the securities you buy. We seldom buy stocks priced higher than $25 per share. One of the main reasons for this is that we like to buy lots of 100 to save on commissions. (Most brokers charge larger commissions for odd lots.) The lower the price, the more quickly you will have enough money saved up to buy 100 shares.

Types of Stock

Spread your investments among industries that are experiencing growth. This diversifies your opportunities and limits your risk. One good source of areas that are ripe for investment is *Value Line*'s list of timely industries. It is also wise to choose industries that at least one of your members is familiar with or interested in. (For more information about choosing stocks, see Chapter 10.)

Keeping Stock in Street Name

In years gone by, investors who bought securities expected to receive stock certificates that they could file away. When they sold a stock, the certificate had to be sent back to the broker.

These days, investors rarely see a stock certificate. Stocks are still registered in an individual's name, but brokers make "book entries," a written or computerized record of each stock transaction. Copies of account activity are sent to them monthly.

If you really want to, you can register stock in a club's name and have the certificates sent to you directly. Make sure that you agree upon a way to secure the certificates, either in a partner's home or in a safety deposit box. This is probably more hassle than it's worth, though.

Another option, the one we prefer, is to purchase stocks in "street name," a service that most brokers will provide free of charge. If stocks are held in street name, you will not have to bother with certificates. Instead, the broker will open an account in the club's name and enter a book entry on every transaction. The club will receive a monthly statement detailing its holdings, their value, and all transactions during the past month.

If a stock is held in street name, dividends are sent to the broker, who should credit them to the club's account. Annual reports and other information are sent to the broker, who should forward them to the club, usually addressed to the financial partner. All stocks held in street name are secured in accounts insured up to $500,000 by the federal government against brokerage fraud or failure. (Of course, you are not insured against losses incurred by drops in the price of the stock.)

The Beardstown Business & Professional Women's Investment Club Partnership Agreement

This agreement of partnership, made as of October 2, 1980, between the undersigned partners and revised as of November 3, 1983.

I. FORMATION OF PARTNERSHIP: The undersigned hereby form a General Partnership in, and in accordance with, the laws of the State of Illinois.

II. NAME OF PARTNERSHIP: The name of the partnership shall be, The Beardstown Business & Professional Women's Investment Club.

III. TERM: The revised partnership shall begin on November 3, 1983. On any anniversary date thereafter, the partners may vote to terminate the partnership. A two-thirds majority shall rule. Assets should be liquidated and disbursed by or before December 31st of the year the vote to terminate is carried.

IV. PURPOSE: The purpose of the partnership shall be to invest the assets of the partnership solely in stocks, bonds, and securities for the education and benefit of the partners.

V. MEETINGS: Periodic meetings shall be held the first Thursday of each month.

VI. CONTRIBUTIONS: The partners will make equal contributions to the partnership on each monthly meeting of $25.00, payable by check or cash in the club's name, to the Financial Partner. Upon the death of a partner, her contribution shall cease.

VII. VALUATION: The current value of the assets and property of the partnership, less the current value of the debts and liabilities of the partnership (hereinafter referred to as "value of the partnership") shall be determined as of the statement date of the broker's monthly statement. The aforementioned date of valuation shall hereinafter be referred to as "valuation date."

VIII. CAPITAL ACCOUNTS: There shall be maintained in the name of each partner a capital account. Any increase or decrease in the value of the partnership on any valuation date shall be credited or debited, respectively, to each partner's capital account, in proportion to the value of each partner's capital account on said date. Each partner's contribution to the partnership shall be credited to that partner's capital account.

IX. MANAGEMENT: Each partner shall participate in the management and conduct of the affairs of the partnership on an equal basis. Decisions shall be made by a two-thirds majority of the members of the partnership, except as stated in Section XIV, which will require a simple majority vote of the partnership members. A written and signed proxy when assigned to a partner in attendance at a meeting shall be considered the vote cast by the absent partner. However, no more than one proxy may be accepted or voted by any partner.

X. SHARING OF PROFITS AND LOSSES: Net profits and losses of the partnership shall inure to, and be borne by, the partners, in proportion to the credit balances in their capital account.

XI. BOOKS OF ACCOUNT: Books of account of the transactions of the partnership shall be kept and be available and open to inspection and examination by any partner on the meeting day.

XII. ANNUAL ACCOUNTING: At the first business meeting of each calendar year, a full and complete account of the condition of the partnership shall be made to the partners.

XIII. BANK ACCOUNT: The partnership will select a bank for the purpose of opening a partnership bank account. Funds deposited in said bank account shall be withdrawn by checks signed by the Financial Partner and any other appointed partners.

XIV. BROKER ACCOUNT: None of the partners of this partnership shall be a broker; however, the partnership may select a broker and enter into such agreements with said broker as required for the purchase or sale of stocks, bonds, and securities. The Appointed Partner or Financial Partner shall perform the ministerial functions of giving orders to the broker covering the purchase or sale of stocks, bonds, and securities for the accounts of the partnership and then only after said purchases or sales have been approved by a majority vote of the partners of this partnership.

XV. NO COMPENSATION: No partner shall be compensated for services rendered to the partnership, except for reimbursement of authorized expenses.

XVI. WITHDRAWAL: Any partner withdrawing from the partnership will receive one of the following treatments, within 60 days of withdrawal, based on the Club valuation as of the last valuation date.

A. BY DEATH OR INCAPACITY: In the event of death, or physical incapacity, or if a partner is unable to participate actively in the partnership for reasons to be approved by 2/3 vote of all the partners, one hundred percent (100%) of said partner's capital account as described in Section VII and VIII of this agreement, less expenses incurred to liquidate assets to satisfy said amount shall be made available for payment to the partner's estate.

1. Partnership may purchase said capital account or sell to any person acceptable to a two-thirds majority of the remaining partners.

2. Partnership may liquidate assets to satisfy said amount.

B. BY VOLUNTARY WITHDRAWAL: A partner may withdraw from the partnership by submitting a withdrawal request to the Senior Partner. She may . . .

1. Sell her capital account, as described in Section VII and VIII of this agreement to the partnership, or to any person acceptable to a two-thirds majority of the remaining partners.

2. Liquidate her account, incurring all expenses of this liquidation and receive 95% of the proceeds.

C. AUTOMATIC WITHDRAWAL: Should a partner be delinquent in her monthly contributions for a period of 61 days, she will automatically be terminated as a partner and will receive an amount equal to 85% of her capital account as described in Sections VII and VIII less the amount of any delinquent contribution and fines as described in Section XVII of this agreement.

1. Partnership may purchase capital account or sell to any person acceptable to a two-thirds majority of remaining partners.

2. Partnership may liquidate assets to satisfy said amount and deduct the expenses from proceeds to the delinquent partner.

XVII. DELINQUENT CONTRIBUTION: Monthly contributions to the partnership are due on each regular monthly meeting. Should a partner be delinquent in her monthly contribution of more than one week, a delinquent fine of $1.00 will be imposed on said partner. Should the delinquency exceed 31 days an additional delinquent fine of $3.00 will be imposed on said partner. Should the delinquency exceed 61 days, the said partner's membership shall be terminated as outlined in Section XVI, Paragraph C of this agreement. Fines shall be deposited in Club's bank account.

XVIII. OFFICERS: The Senior Partner, Junior Partner, Recording Partner, and the Financial Partner will be elected annually during the regular October meeting. The newly elected officers shall assume the duties of their respective offices at the November meeting of each year. Officers may succeed themselves in the same office.

It shall be the duty of the Senior Partner to preside at meetings; appoint a parliamentarian; appoint committees, and oversee club activities.

The Junior Partner shall assume the duties of the Senior Partner when the Senior Partner is absent or temporarily unable to carry out her duties. In addition, the Junior Partner will be responsible for the educational program of the partnership.

The Recording Partner shall keep a record of club activities and report on previous meetings.

The Financial Partner shall place, buy and sell orders on instruction from the membership, collect and disburse funds, maintain a set of books covering the club's financial operations, assets, and members' shares, and issue receipts to partners for their deposits. She shall prepare an annual statement of liquidating value and prepare proper tax forms.

XIX. AUDITING: Within thirty (30) days prior to the annual accounting, an auditing committee comprised of two (2) non-officer partners, appointed by the Senior Partner, shall inspect the partnership records in conjunction with the Financial Partner.

XX. AMENDMENTS: The partnership may, at any time, amend this partnership agreement by a two-thirds majority vote of the partners, with the exception of this section (Section XX), which will require a unanimous vote.

XXI. DEBT: At no time will the total debt of the partnership exceed an amount equal to 5% of the monthly contributions of the partnership.

XXII. FORBIDDEN ACTS: No partner shall:

A. Have the right or authority to bind or obligate the partnership to any extent whatsoever with regard to any matter outside the scope of the partnership business.

B. Assign, transfer, pledge, mortgage or sell all or part of her interest in the partnership to any other partner, except as stated in Section XVI B, paragraph 2.

C. Purchase an investment for the partnership where less than the full purchase price is paid for same.

D. Use the partnership name, credit or property for other than partnership purposes.

E. Do any act detrimental to the best interest of the

partnership or which would make it impossible to carry on the business or affairs of the partnership.

This agreement of partnership is hereby declared and shall be binding upon the respective heirs, executors, administrators and personal representatives of their parties.

IN WITNESS WHEREOF, the parties have set their hands and seal the year and the day first above written.

When Wall Street Visits Peoria:
Investing from the World Around You

The world around you can be your best source of investment tips, even if you live in a small town. Keep your eyes open for exciting new business and for missteps by established companies—both can signal rises or drops in a stock before the rest of the market notices.

Prudential Securities vice president Ralph Acampora, a frequent guest on Louis Rukeyser's public television show "Wall Street Week," discovered the investment value of small-town living last fall during a trip to Peoria, Illinois, where he met Shirley Gross, one of our charter members.

Acampora, a speaker at an NAIC investors' fair that Gross attended, asked her about the club's investments. "I don't think I'd hold on to that one any longer," Ralph said, when he heard that one of the club's favorite stocks was Wal-Mart. He was unenthusiastic about the company's prospects.

Shirley replied, respectfully of course, that she disagreed. "Every time I go Wal-Mart, I have to drive around the parking lot looking for a parking space. Even spaces reserved for the handicapped are full," she said. "When I go inside, the aisles are blocked by people pushing shopping carts, and the shopping carts are full."

"Have you ever been in a Wal-Mart?" she asked. Ralph, who lives in New York City—one of the few places in the United States where there aren't any Wal-Marts—confessed that he hadn't.

The next morning Ralph walked a few blocks from the hotel where he was staying to a nearby Wal-Mart store. About an hour later, he returned to the hotel with his arms so full of bags he could hardly walk. "Do you see this?" he said excitedly to Brian Pier, treasurer of the Heart of Illinois Regional NAIC Council, the first person he ran into at the hotel. "I bought a whole bag of shirts. They are the same brand I buy in New York, but they cost half the price!" Ralph was so loaded down with packages, Brian had to help him up to his room. And the analyst had changed his mind about investing in Wal-Mart.

Ralph had done what the Beardstown Ladies do as often as they can—make their own firsthand observations of companies they are following. Ralph's personal shopping trip was more instructive than all the company presentations he had attended and analysts' reports that had crossed his desk. At the time, Wal-Mart stock was trading at 23½; now it is up to 27½.*

*At closing, March 16, 1994.

4. Meeting for Fun and Profit: How to Do Both

Starting a meeting with a poem or prayer puts the group in a friendly and reflective mood. The senior partner, who presides over the meetings while she is in office, sets the tone. During the year that Maxine Thomas was senior partner, for instance, "she never got too serious about anything," says Hazel Lindahl. "Meetings were just like a family talking about something." Other senior partners have been slightly more formal.

Most important is keeping meetings lively, educational and efficient. They do not need to last longer than an hour and a half, and partners should leave feeling their time was well spent.

Reading the Minutes

Once the senior partner calls the meeting to order, the first item on the agenda should be reading the minutes of the last gathering. The recording partner should ask members to make any corrections or additions—they are rare—and then to approve the minutes with a voice vote. (One time Carnell missed a meeting when she was the recording partner. At the next meeting she read the minutes of the meeting she had missed, which were written by somebody else. When she came to the word "condom," which was part of our discussion about Gillette's products in the light of the AIDS epidemic, Carnell thought surely there must be some mistake and read "condominiums" instead. We all had a good laugh over that one.)

Treasurer's Report

Next comes the treasurer's report by the financial partner, which should include any bank and brokerage account balances and the current value of the club's portfolio.

Club Business

The treasurer's report should be followed by club business, such as reading correspondence from other clubs or discussing plans for attending upcoming educational seminars or considering applications from potential new members.

Stock Information Sheet

Before we begin, each member takes out her personal copy of a Stock Information Sheet, a format we developed that is popular with other clubs. (See sample, p. 36.) It lists each stock that we own, the number of shares held, the cost per share at the time of purchase, and the total cost to the club. Every sheet has at least six columns, each representing a different month, that can be filled in at each meeting. We track each stock's price, price-earnings ratio, timeliness, safety, and industry rank.

One member should be responsible for gathering this information on all of the club's holdings on the day of the meeting and reading it aloud to the group so that the others can fill it in on their own sheets. Shirley Gross, who subscribes to *The Wall Street Journal* and *Value Line*, does that for us. If you don't have a partner who subscribes to these publications, you might choose someone who has easy access to a library or bank that subscribes to both.

The Stock Information Sheet was designed to give everyone an easy-to-read overview of how the club's portfolio is performing. As we're filling in the numbers, it triggers an early warning if a stock's timeliness or safety has fallen too far or price-earnings ratio seems too high. Filling these sheets out as a group is a quick, efficient way to review your portfolio every month.

Stock Reports

Once the latest numbers are entered, each partner takes a turn reporting on the stock she is following. You can do it in any order, but we stick to alphabetical by company name. An individual stock report will mention any significant new development that occurred in the last month, such as a new product introduction, highlights from a quarterly report, or a potential merger.

Some members become big fans of the company they are following. "You're always hoping it will go up," says Ann Corley. One night Doris Edwards, who follows Hershey's, brought its new product, Hugs, a Kiss-shaped candy that combines white and milk chocolate, to our meeting so we could all have a taste.

Treats add to the enjoyment of the evening, of course, but sampling products by companies in which you are investing serves a serious purpose, too: It adds personal insight to the

Stock Information Sheet (sample)

# of shares	security	price/share	total cost	MAY — price/share, p.e. ratio/industry rank, timeliness/safety	JUNE — price/share, p.e. ratio/industry rank, timeliness/safety	JULY — price/share, p.e. ratio/industry rank, timeliness/safety
100	Cooper Tire and Rubber	25.63	2562.44	26 / 20.2/23 / 3/3		
100	Cracker Barrel	26.14	2614.02	24 / 26/15 / 2/3		
125	A.G. Edwards	9.76	1220.16	17⅞ / 6.15/18 / 3/3		
100	Glaxo Holdings	8.92	892.28	17⅛ / 12.6/69 / 3/3		
100	Hershey's	32.72	3272.32	43⅝ / 14.9/58 / 4/1		
100	Merck	42.06	4206.42	30⅛ / 12.1/42 / 3/1		
200	McDonald's	14.69	2937.83	59½ / 17.2/8 / 2/1		
100	Pepsico	32.88	3287.77	34 / 16.4/6 / 2/2		

Stock Information Sheet (sample)

# of shares	security	price/ share	total cost	MAY price/share, p.e. ratio, industry rank, timeliness, safety	JUNE price/share, p.e. ratio, industry rank, timeliness, safety	JULY price/share, p.e. ratio, industry rank, timeliness, safety
100	Quaker Oats	72.74	7274.19	64⅜ / 13.9/53 / 3/2		
300	RPM	6.99	2096.74	18⅛ / 18.5/46 / 3/3		
100	Rubbermaid	32.20	3220.03	26¼ / 17.6/15 / 3/2		
150	Rollins	11.11	1666.63	29.38 / 19/16 / 2/2		
150	VeriFone	21.37	3204.97	17¾ / 20/N.A. / N.A.		
300	Wolverine Worldwide	8.32	2495.33	28¼ / 18.5/71 / 1/3		
200	Wal-Mart	15.42	3084.64	25 / 20.3/34 / 2/2		
100	Waste Management	32.78	3359.14	26½ / 16.4/73 / 4/3		

available information. For instance, if the Hugs hadn't tasted good to us, and the candy was supposed to be a key contributor to profits, we might have been concerned. (To the contrary, we thought they were delicious, which heightened our already high level of enthusiasm for Hershey's.)

Stock Selection Committee Report— Buy, Sell, or Hold?

Next comes the Stock Selection Committee report, which many find the most interesting portion of the meeting because that is when stocks are bought and sold. The committee—composed of two or three partners who volunteer to study and recommend stocks until one is selected—presents stocks that they think the club should consider buying beyond those we already hold. One committee member should give a succinct account—going over price, price-earnings ratio, beta, timeliness, safety, and other important indicators—that explains why the stock deserves consideration. A case is more strongly made if the committee has chosen the stock after comparing it to two other companies in the same industry.

Example: When we considered buying PepsiCo in December 1991, the committee compared it to Coca-Cola and A&W. Coca-Cola came out ahead on a number of Value Line ratings, including timeliness and safety. But ultimately we chose PepsiCo because we liked the fact that the company, owner of Kentucky Fried Chicken, Taco Bell, and other fast-food chains, and maker of pasta, was so diversified.

Once a stock has been presented, discussion should be opened. If a buy recommendation is being discussed, the group should compare the proposed stock to the holdings the club already has, since it might be better to spend money on additional shares of stocks that you already own. This is also the time when motions to sell current holdings are brought up. Once you have a motion on the floor, another member should second it before there is a vote.

If we do not have enough money to buy anything, sometimes we postpone the Stock Selection Committee's report. We always hold off on voting to buy stock until we have money on hand. If the committee has investigated several stocks, but hasn't found anything it wants to recommend, the members may still give brief reports on the stocks that they studied. Sometimes they recommend that we continue to follow a stock because, while it isn't what we are looking for right then, it holds promise for the future.

After a buy or sell motion is carried, we disband the current Stock Selection Committee and ask for new volunteers. Committee participation greatly improves one's understanding of the stock market, and we urge you to rotate this responsibility among all members. It only adds a few hours of work during the month.

Educational Presentation

Next the club should set aside time for an educational presentation. The junior partner usually plans a 15- to 20-minute discussion of some educational value, such as reporting on interesting articles in the financial press, leading a discussion of a helpful NAIC investment tool (such as the Stock Comparison Guide), or explaining a financial term. Sometimes the junior partner will assign some reading or a worksheet that the whole group can go over together at a following meeting. For example, we were all asked to come to our February 1994 meeting with a Stock Selection Guide filled out on the stock that we are following for the club.

Many groups neglect to set aside time for education during their meeting. "A couple of our members were invited to visit a nearby club and all they did was eat," says Buffy Tillitt-Pratt, laughing. "We think that is a big mistake." "There is always more to learn," says Ann Corley, who has been a member since 1985.

New Business

At the end of the meeting, set aside a few minutes for new business—making important announcements and selecting the time and place for the next meeting.

If you keep your meeting time regular (we meet the first Thursday of every month), you will encounter fewer scheduling conflicts. Meeting at different restaurants can add to the fun, but make sure they have a meeting room large enough to accommodate the serious part of your get-together.

When members leave, they should feel that, in addition to charting how their profits have grown, they have added to their storehouse of knowledge. If your members are as good-natured as ours, they will have shared a few laughs as well.

Sample Minutes

The Beardstown BPW Investment Club met at the First Evangelical Lutheran Church for their regular meeting. Senior Partner Maxine Thomas called the meeting to order at 7:05 P.M. There were 14 members and two guests present.

Maxine introduced the guests and read a short poem. The minutes were read and approved.

Financial Partner Betty Sinnock gave the following treasurer's report: First State Bank balance—$1,206.62; A. G. Edwards account balance—$196.10; Portfolio value—$65,715.45.

Betty read correspondence from Betty Taylor, national director of NAIC. Shirley read correspondence from Jean Buie of Ashland School, where several of our members have gone to speak to students.

Stock prices were filled in on our stock information sheets and individual stock reports were given. The stock selection committee—Buffy Tillitt-Pratt, Ann Corley, and Margaret Houchins—presented the stocks: Old Kent Financial, Merck & Co., and Kyear Industrials. Buffy suggested we consider purchasing more shares of Wal-Mart even though the price is high because she has learned that its stock is due to split. Ann Brewer made a motion to sell Calgon Carbon stock, seconded by Margaret. After discussion, the vote was unanimous.

Carnell Korsmeyer made a motion for Betty to prepare a stock evaluation on Merck & Co. and if it is in the "maybe" or "buy" range (as indicated by NAIC's Stock Selection Guide), to purchase 100 shares. The motion was seconded by Shirley Gross and carried.

Betty made a motion to sell 77 shares of Lawter International, seconded by Buffy. Motion carried.

The new Stock Selection Committee, appointed by senior partner Maxine Thomas, will include Ruth Huston and Ann Brewer.

New business: Maxine announced the dates and times of two upcoming Heart of Illinois Council meetings. New NAIC investment manuals were given out.

The next club meeting will be held in the Lutheran Church at 7:00 P.M. on February 4, 1993. Meeting was adjourned at 8:35 P.M.

Recording partner, Margaret A. Houchins

5. Hiring a Broker: Selection Guidelines

Not every investment club needs or wants a full-service broker. For one thing, they are expensive, charging roughly 3% to 5% of the cost of a trade in commission, which quickly dampens your returns. Secondly, because brokers make their money by executing trades, it can be difficult to find one who caters to the conservative, long-term investment philosophy central to a club's financial success.

That said, it has been our experience that a broker who enthusiastically supports a club can be an invaluable asset. Our broker, Homer Rieken, of A. G. Edwards's Springfield office, has helped us from the start. Over the years, he has assisted us with organizational questions, given us stock recommendations (all of which we have followed up with our own research), and spoken at our meetings. He has also added to our fun by giving us a tour of his office and taking us out to dinner during the Christmas holidays. A firm believer in the educational value of investment clubs, he has cheered us on as word of our success has spread. (Naturally, the publicity has done him some good, too. Homer has received calls from people all over the country who want to be his clients.)

In addition to securing profitable advice and counsel, using a full-service broker adds some convenience to the group's operating procedures. Such a broker can be the custodian of your securities, collect dividends and keep them in your account until they are reinvested, and forward stockholder information. Your broker will also send a monthly statement of your account to the club's financial partner, who should disseminate it to the members at each meeting.

If you are considering working with a full-service broker, be sure to get recommendations from past clients. Even if he or she is referred to you by someone whose judgment you trust, take the time to interview the broker in person. Remember: a broker works for you, and you need to establish a comfortable working relationship. Is he accessible? Does he willingly answer questions? Are the answers clear? Yes should be the reply to all of these questions, whether you are looking for a broker to work with you or your investment club.

If you are looking for a broker for the club, make sure he is comfortable working with an investment club. Is he familiar with clubs and how they operate? Does he agree with your club's investment philosophy?

The personal attention given by a full-service broker is not useful to every club or individual, so you might investigate several less expensive alternatives. Discount brokers, such as Prime Vest Brokerage Service and Zigler Thrift, for

---

Checklist:
How to Choose a Broker

1. Get several recommendations from people whose judgment you trust.
2. Interview each candidate in person. Make sure they are accessible, have time to spend, and are comfortable working with an investment club.
3. Ask about investment philosophy: How do they invest their own money? Are they comfortable holding on to stocks for a long period? If not, go elsewhere.
4. Get the names and numbers of several references. Call them before you make your final decision.
5. Compare the fee structure and services offered with those of discount and deep discount brokers. Do the extra services justify the added cost?

---

instance, generally offer lower fees. Make sure to ask about their minimum charges, because if you only have several hundred dollars to invest every month, the charges may not be any lower than those of a full-service broker.

Discount brokers execute buy and sell orders but generally do not provide advice. Mercer Inc. tracks firms with the lowest commissions. (Contact them at 379 W. Broadway, Suite 400, New York, NY 10012.)

Another possibility is to work with a full-service broker when you need guidance, and a discount broker when you do not. (Be sure to buy a stock you have picked with the help of a full-service broker from that broker, since that is how he makes his income.)

You can also limit your commission costs by trading via NAIC's Low-Cost Investment Plan, which allows you to invest in more than 100 companies for only a $5 service fee per company. Buy one share through NAIC and make all subsequent purchases through the company's dividend reinvestment agent. The only disadvantage of this stock-purchasing method is that you are limited to the companies that participate in the investment plan.

Selecting a broker is not unlike selecting stocks: you're much better off if you do your homework first.

6. What Happens When Someone Leaves the Club?

If your club is fortunate enough to stay together for an extended period of years, you are likely to lose a member or two along the way. We have lost quite a few members—one to death, two to financial hardship, and others for various personal reasons.

Paying off a club member who withdraws can be accomplished several different ways, but the first step is to determine the value of that member's share of the portfolio. If your club adopts the NAIC's Unit Value System (see below) to track members' investments, this should be a relatively easy task.

Once you know the amount required, you may take the

NAIC'S Valuation Unit System*

NAIC's Valuation Unit System is a method for keeping track of partners' investments in a club. A system similar to those used by mutual funds, it is a useful way to track members' shares, which may vary over time as charter members quit and new members join.

Because a club's assets fluctuate with the market value of the stocks it holds, its assets must be tabulated on a regular basis. This is generally done by the financial partner a day or two before the monthly meeting. The "Valuation Statement" lists the assets of the club at their market value as of the valuation date. Most clubs use the closing price of listed securities and the bid price of over-the-counter issues.

Then follow these steps to establish a unit system:

1. Establish an amount to be the unit value of ownership in the club. The common amount is $10 for one unit. Each member's account record should list the amount of cash deposits and the "valuation units" credited to her account. A member's liquidating value is easily computed at any time by multiplying the member's total valuation units by the established dollar amount of a unit.
   Example: If a member has 250 units (each worth $10) credited to her account, the liquidating value of her account would be $2,500.

2. Divide the total value of the Valuation Statement by $10.00 and take the quotient as the number of valuation units in the club.
   Example: If the Valuation Statement total is $3,000, the total number of units would be $3,000 divided by $10, or 300.

3. Allocate these valuation units to your members.
   a. When everyone has an equal interest, divide the total number of valuation units by the total number of members to determine the valuation units for each member.
   Example: If the club has 15 members who have invested the same amount of money in the club, and 300 units, each member would be credited with 20 units. The liquidating value of each member's portion at that time would be $200.

b. When interests are unequal, calculate the percentage of the value of each member's account to the total value of the club. Determine the number of each member's valuation units by applying her percentage of ownership to the total number of valuation units.

Example: Let's suppose that a club has a total value of $3,000, 300 units, and 15 members. Thirteen original members own a total of 90% of the club and two new members have joined with intial investments of $150 each, or 5% of the valuation of the club. Each charter member should be credited with 20.76 units (90% of 300 units, divided by 13). The two new members should each be credited with 15 units (5% of 300 units).

4. After determining the total number of valuation units and the number for each member, with the value set at $10, you are ready to receive the current month's receipts. For each $10 you received at this time, add one valuation unit to each member's account and to the grand total of valuation units.

Example: Continuing from the above example, let's say monthly dues are $20. After collecting dues, each of the thirteen members would have 22.76 units. Each new member would have 17 units. The new total of valuation units would be 330.

5. At the next meeting, divide the total of your liquidating statement by the new total of valuation units, thus determining the value of one unit. Divide $10 by the new unit value; the resulting figure will be the number of units each $10 deposited in the club will purchase at that meeting.

Example: Assume that the value of the club's assets has risen to $3,500. Divide $3,500 by 330 units. The result is $10.60. Divide $10 by $10.60 to get .9433. This is the number of units each $10 deposited in the club will be worth. Each member who contributes dues of $20 should be credited with 1.886 units.

6. From this point forward, continue to accumulate valuation units as shown in Step 5.

*(Adapted from Chapter 20 of NAIC's Investors Manual. For additional information on the Valuation Unit System, consult this chapter or NAIC's Club Accounting Software.)

money out of the club's coffers, or you may invite a new member to contribute an amount equal to the departing member's share.

Some clubs require that new members start with the same amount of money that charter members have invested, but this can be financially prohibitive. Our only requirement is that a new member start with an initial amount of $100. New partners, however, can make contributions at any time up to the value that charter members have.

One of our newer members, Buffy Tillitt-Pratt, who is a real estate broker, chose to buy out the departing member's share, which was $1,200 at the time. To keep records complete, Buffy paid her share to the club, and the club paid an equal amount to the departing member.

Another time we paid off a departing member by selling some of our stock. We sold 50 shares of RPM and 100 shares of Zero Corp., which covered her share, and paid her in cash.

Another method that may be more advantageous for both the club and departing member is to pay her off by transferring securities to the member's ownership, which is not a taxable transaction. To accomplish this, you must send a letter to your broker stating the time of transfer, number of shares, and the name of the member. If the withdrawing member prefers cash, she then may instruct the broker to sell the stock. The club simply writes off the stock, deducting the value of the member's account from its income at the end of the year. The stock is now the sole property of the departing member.

If your club sells stocks to pay a withdrawing member, the remaining partners must pay taxes on the profits from the stock. Consequently, from a tax perspective the partnership will do better if it sells stocks at a loss. If the club is transferring stocks, the opposite is true. Writing off stocks held at a profit keeps taxes down.

Part Two

INVESTING THE BEARDSTOWN LADIES' WAY

Getting Ready

7. The Key to Our Strategy: The Stock Market— Two Centuries of Growth

In the 310 years since Wall Street's course was laid out in lower Manhattan, it has developed from a place overrun by pirates and slave traders to the heart of the financial world. Home for more than two centuries to the country's premier stock exchange and legions of stock brokers, traders, and analysts, it has come to symbolize the promise of free enterprise.

Wall Street was already a haven for commercial activity by 1792, the year 24 gentlemen met beneath a buttonwood tree as "brokers for the purchase and sale of public stocks," the precursor to the New York Stock Exchange (NYSE). The exchange was first organized to allow individuals to increase their capital in exchange for providing funds to private enterprise. This purpose remains the same today.

The 24 original gentlemen began trading stocks two years after the first American turnpike was built, and the exchange has operated almost without interruption throughout the economic and political history of the nation.

Not that it hasn't been affected by political events. Worldwide panic at the outset of World War I caused the stock exchange to shut down for several months in 1914. The Dow Jones Industrial Average, an index of 30 major stocks traded on the NYSE, dropped 15% in just two weeks in 1915, reflecting concern about U.S.-German relations and the sinking of the *Lusitania*. It skidded another 33% after the United States entered the war in 1917. More staggering was the freefall between February 1931 and July 1932, when the industrial average plunged almost 79% while the country suffered through a severe economic depression.

More recently, OPEC's oil embargo, announced on October 19, 1973, helped drive the Dow down 16% in three months and 39% in 12 months. By December 1974, many blue-chip stocks had fallen between 50% and 90%. On October 19, 1987, the Dow dropped 508 points, its largest one-day decline.

But despite economic plunges, the market has always roared back—and ascended even higher. Between September 1953 and December 1955, for instance, the Dow Jones Industrial Average climbed 292 points, or 107%. The Dow dropped 23% on Black Monday in October 1987, but since then it has risen 121%, to over 3500.

The market's history of outstanding growth is undeniable when you look at its record since the beginning of the century. Standard & Poor's 500, an index of 500 major stocks listed on the NYSE, has plotted an overall upward trend, averaging an annual 9% return rate and outperforming most other investments. Its record is twice as good as that of corporate bonds (4.4%), Treasury bills (3.3%), and inflation (3.3%). In

When the Dow Falls, It's Time to Go Shopping

What goes down, must come up. It's contrary to intuition, but it's been true of the stock market for 200 years. The trick is to remember this truism when stock prices embark on one of their inevitable skids.

Stocks have taken numerous tumbles in the 10 years we have been trading as a club, the most notable of which was the 508-point drop on October 19, 1987. During any fall, especially one that severe, the temptation for inexperienced investors is to get out as quickly as possible, to sell shares and take money back before its value diminishes any further.

But more experienced—and successful—investors steel their nerves . . . and go shopping. Depressed markets with bargain-basement prices are the most opportune times to increase your holdings. After the drop in 1987, "we bought as many stocks as we could before prices started to go up again," recalls Betty Sinnock. "We wished we had more money to invest because there were so many stocks we were anxious to buy."

At our September meeting, Lillian Ellis told the group about analysts who compared the current economy to the 1920s, noting that most experts predicted that a market drop at this time would not be as severe as the Depression. We held on to our investments, which were worth $24,598.

By November 7, the value of our portfolio had dropped to $17,326, a 28.7% loss from a month earlier, but we did not panic. Instead, we bought 25 shares of A. G. Edwards, adding to the 75 shares we already owned, and 40 shares of Rollins, a consumer services company specializing in lawn care and home security services. Our members were so anxious to take advantage of bargain prices that we voted to pay our December dues early to have sufficient funds for our purchases.

And our eagerness paid off when we tallied our returns. A. G. Edwards, which we bought at 18 1/2, split twice and closed at the end of December 1993 at 29 7/8, giving us a capital gain of 79%, or an annual return of 33.8%.

Rollins, which we bought at 16 5/8, had a 3-for-2 split and closed on December 31, 1993, at 26 1/4, giving us an 84% gain, or an annual return of 22.81%.

Dow Jones Industrial Average 1920-1993

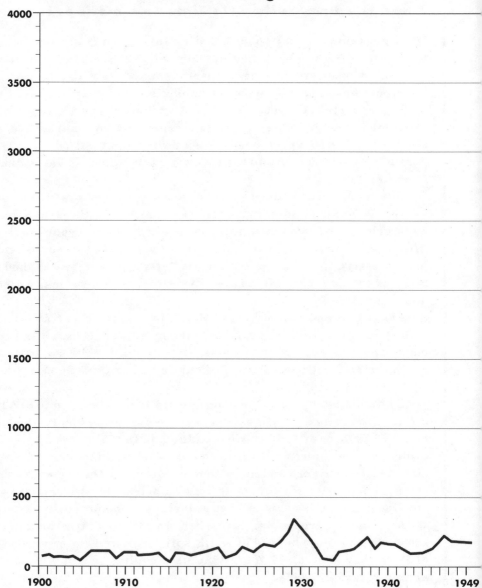

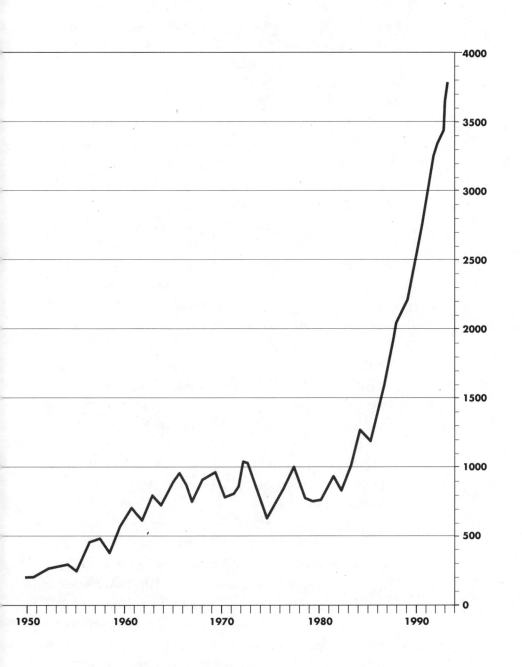

fact, after inflation, Treasury bills provide a zero return, in contrast to stocks, which have a return of over 6%. The lesson of history is clear: the stock market consistently provides investors with opportunities that are difficult to match elsewhere.

Over the years, investors have financed some remarkable businesses and reaped some impressive rewards. McDonald's, for one, was first sold to the public in 1965 for $22.50 a share. Ten shares, after 10 splits, by September 1993 would have multiplied to 1,859 shares worth $96,000.

As American business has expanded, the Dow Jones Industrial Average has climbed and the market for stocks has flourished. In 1812, the NYSE had 28 members and listed 30 securities. Its trading hours were minimal: from 10:30 A.M. to 12 noon and from 1:00 to 2:00 P.M. Today the exchange lists 2,984 securities and trading hours extend from 9:30 A.M. to 4:00 P.M. It is not unusual for 300 million shares to trade in a single day, up from 6 million shares just 30 years ago.

The number of Americans participating in the market's growth has mushroomed as well. During the Depression years, only 1% of Americans owned stock. Now nearly three-quarters of the U.S. population owns shares of corporations, either directly or indirectly through pension plans, mutual savings, bank accounts, and life insurance policies that are invested in the market.

Despite these numbers, most American adults—three out of four, a large portion of them women—have never purchased a stock or mutual fund on their own. An estimated 80% of women will have to take charge of their own finances at some point in their lives. Yet a recent survey by Oppenheimer Funds found that while women play a major role in the day-to-day management of household finances, paying bills and maintaining the checkbook, they have been less involved with long-term planning issues like investments or retirement.

Based on firsthand experience, we know that stocks offer equal opportunities to both men and women, young and old, who are anxious to expand their capital and contribute to the financing of free enterprise here and abroad. The market has a history of alternating rises with dips, there's no doubt about it. But investors who are prepared with a basic understanding of the market, and treat stocks as a serious, long-term investment, are likely to be rewarded with a return that is hard to match elsewhere.

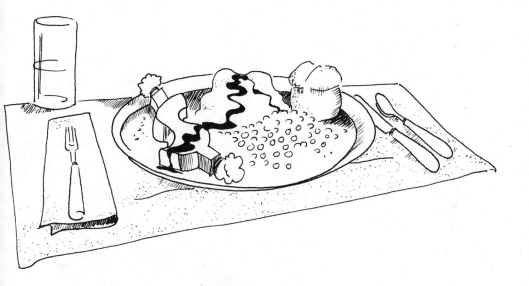

8. Assessing Your Financial Picture: Getting Ready to Invest

Now that you know how to set up a club and the key to our strategy, it's time to assess your own financial picture and begin to invest.

The Financial Plan

Without planning, it's nearly impossible to increase your wealth. By contrast, "poverty needs no plan," writes Napoleon Hill, the author of motivational books inspired by Andrew Carnegie. Whatever your situation—whether you are trying to scrape enough money together to cover your expenses or wondering where to invest excess income—

financial planning is the foundation of a sound economic future. The earlier you begin planning, the more secure your future will be.

Except for our investments with the club, each Beardstown Lady manages her own finances, either in cooperation with her husband or on her own. The investments we choose to make as individuals run the gamut from bank certificates of deposit to real estate to stocks and mutual funds. But there is one thing we all have in common: every one of us has a financial plan.

Like a map, a financial plan tells you how to get where you want to go. Crucial to a profitable economic journey is first pinpointing where you are now, and then deciding where it is you want to go. What is your current financial situation? How much money do you want to save and when do you need it? Only when you have answered these questions can you evaluate the many available routes and choose the one that suits you best—taking into account safety, directness, and speed.

Calculating Your Net Worth

The best way to evaluate your current situation is to determine your net worth. Here's how to do it in three easy steps:

1. List the current value of your *assets*, which are anything of significant value that you own, including your home; other real estate; cars; financial investments such as stocks and bonds; savings accounts; the market value of your cars; artwork and other collectibles; the value of your business, if you own one; home furnishings; clothing; books; trusts and any other large-ticket items.

2. Calculate your *liabilities*, or debts. This list should include mortgages, car loans, student loans, personal loans, and credit card debt.

3. Subtract liabilities from assets and you've got a good estimate of your present net worth. Try it— most people are pleasantly surprised at the way their assets add up!

With prudent purchases, investments, and savings, net worth is a number that you should see grow over time. The next time you are weighing a big purchase, take into consideration its likely contribution to your personal bottom line. Expensive clothes, for instance, will probably depreciate in value over time, while an original oil painting is more likely to grow (but don't count on it). A $15,000 mini-van will only drop in value once it's driven off the new car lot, while a similar amount spent upgrading your kitchen will add value to your house.

Setting Goals

Now it's time to draw on your imaginative powers. Visualize yourself in the near future. What about in 10 years? Some questions to ask yourself: Where do you want to live? What do you want to be doing? How much is that likely to cost?

After you have finished dreaming—and be sure to allow yourself plenty of time—it is time to come back to earth and make a list of your goals for the future. Though you should be guided by your dreams, this is a time for prioritizing and pruning. You are more likely to realize your ambitions if you choose ones that are practical.

Next to each goal write your estimate of the time you have to save for that goal and the amount you need to save.

Example: Saving for a down payment on a house, 5 years, $20,000.

Estimating costs can be difficult, but David Kliff, president of Personal Financial Advisors in Arlington Heights, Illinois, offers the following guidelines:

If you are saving for educational expenses, determine the current cost of the school you are aiming for and add 8% for every year until enrollment.

Example: If you are saving for tuition so you can send your son to a nearby two-year college and the current cost is $5,000 per year, you need to save $10,000 plus 8% for every year between now and when he is expected to enroll. If you expect him to start college five years from now, for instance, you would need to save a total of $15,281. Divide that by 60 months, and you can see that your goal should be generating roughly $225 per month through savings and/ or investments.

Retirement planning must take into account the way you want to live—in a smaller apartment, in the home where you currently live, or perhaps dividing your time between condominiums in two different climates. Once you envision your future lifestyle as best you can, then you need to estimate what your expenses might be. Often people use 75% of their current costs as a general guideline for what their retirement budget should be. Add to that 6% for every year until you reach retirement age.

Kliff notes: If selling your home when you retire is part of your plan, remember that your house is likely to appreciate 6% a year between now and then, when figuring future assets. (During the last 10 years, residential housing appreciated an average of 4.4% a year, according to the National Association of Realtors. Between 1945 and 1993 the yearly average was 7.2%.)

Getting Where You Want to Go

Now that you're ready to invest and you've set your goals, it's time to choose the best route to your desired destination. But first things first. How much fuel have you got? You need to take a close look at your cash flow.

Add up your monthly net income (after taxes) plus any other income you get from real estate or other investments.

Next, draw up a monthly budget so you have a realistic view of your expenses. If there is anything you can cut out this is a good time to do so.

Subtract your expenses from your income and you've got a good idea of what you have to work with. If you have nothing left over, then you have to take a second look at your budget, this time with an eye toward economizing. How about skipping one night out at the movies each month and watching TV instead?

Insurance and Savings

Before even considering various investment options for your surplus, you need to evaluate your insurance coverage. *Life insurance* coverage should be sufficient to care for your dependents until they can support themselves should you pre-decease them. *Health insurance* should be in place to cover you and your family for routine health care and medical emergencies. And *disability insurance* should provide you with the security of enough income to support yourself and dependents if you are suddenly unable to work.

You also need to make certain you have a healthy savings account. "Study diligently your capital requirements, and fortify yourself fully to cover possible setbacks, because you can absolutely count on meeting setbacks," John D. Rocke-

Teaching New Investors Old Tricks:
Passing Along Wisdom

People often wonder why members of a private partnership with an outstanding track record of enviable returns would want to share the names of the stocks in their portfolio, much less the details of their method, with anyone else. Scores of people ask us why we do this. Why give away your secrets, first in a video and now in a book? Why do many of your members volunteer to speak in front of so many other investment clubs?

During our 10 years together, we have benefited from the wisdom and experience of others: from NAIC and its leaders; from more experienced and better-known investors who believed in and practiced investing in fundamentals long before we discovered it; from professionals, like our broker, who have taken time with us and given us guidance when we needed it.

In sharing what we have learned with as many people as will listen, we take our inspiration from Tom O'Hara, chairman of NAIC, who has always freely told whoever asked what his club was investing in. "There are plenty of stocks to go around," is the short answer that many of our members give. But there is much more to it than that.

The more people who can invest successfully in the stock market, the better off we all are. Investors win and American business wins. George Nicholson, chairman of NAIC's advisory board, put it well:

> Capitalism can exist only as equity money is made available to business—small, medium, and large—in all areas here and abroad. Capitalism will work better if people
>
> **(a)** understand investing,
> **(b)** are educated to do so successfully, and
> **(c)** intelligently provide capital to expanding industries.
>
> Investment education is essential to good citizenship in the modern world.

Much of our educational outreach is through our work with the Heart of Illinois NAIC Regional Council. Betty Sinnock, our financial partner and an NAIC national board member, frequently leads seminars for investment clubs in central Illinois. Our members have also spoken before many local civic groups and to several local high school classes.

Many of us also conduct personal campaigns with our grandchildren, trying to get them to begin thinking about saving and investing. You are never too old to start—we have demonstrated that—and you are never too young, either.

feller advised people setting up new businesses. The same advice holds true for people managing their personal affairs.

Most planners recommend having three to six months of expenses in reserve. Your savings should be kept in an account that is easily accessible, such as a certificate of deposit (CD), a short-term bond fund, or a money market account. These are all liquid, safe investments. (There can be a penalty for early withdrawal of a CD, however.)

Savings and insurance in place? Then it is time to consider your investment options. "Financial planning is like a wheel with a hub," advises Kliff. "If it's missing a couple of spokes, it won't work well. You have to have a coordinated strategy."

Deciding Where to Invest

Investments should be selected based on your goals and tolerance for risk. Generally, the higher the return, the more the risk. Will you be happy with a 10% pre-tax return? If you want something higher, are you willing to take on additional risk?

Example: Let's say you have an eight-year-old daughter whom you expect to attend college in 10 years. Expenses at the college you would like to send her to are $10,000 a year, for a total of $40,000. At an 8% annual inflation rate, you *would need a total of $86,357 in nine years. If you have $40,000 to invest today, you should eliminate bonds, cash, and CDs because they will not give you the return you need. Currently, long-term bonds and CDs only yield a return of between 6% and 7%; the return on cash is closer to 4%. Instead, it would probably be wisest to invest in growth stocks or growth stock mutual funds, which have histori- cally earned an average annual return of close to 10%.*

If, on the other hand, you have $2,500 that is designated for no particular purpose and you simply want to see it grow as quickly as possible, you might consider a fund that invests only in technology stocks, for instance, a sector that has the possibility for rapid growth, though it is more risky than a more diversified fund.

Be sure to thoroughly investigate the potential risks and rewards of an investment before making any decision. The mistake many investors make is spending more time picking out a pair of shoes than plotting their financial future.

Monitoring Your Progress

Once you develop a plan, whatever it is, you need to monitor your progress to make sure you are going forward. You may need to make adjustments based on performance and your own changing goals.

If your investments are not generating the return you had expected based on your research, perhaps you need to change your strategy. This is the time when it is particularly important to be as objective as possible and leave your ego out of it. If you did your research ahead of time and made your best guess, there is no one to blame. No one—not you, not the most experienced broker or financial planner, not the wisest economist—can predict the future. For a little perspective, you may want to consult an objective third party, an estate planner, a broker, or some experienced investor whom you trust. You may need to reexamine your options, and pick another route to your destination. On the other hand, you may need to exercise some patience and give your investment more time to grow.

Whatever the advice, it is important to remember that investments are a means to an end, not an end in themselves.

Tools

9. Tools of the Trade and How Things Work

To the uninitiated, stock tables may appear to be just a jumble of numbers, but once you have invested in a stock, they make for riveting reading. When you learn the simple art of how to read the tables, you will have mastered one of the essential tools used by professional and amateur investors alike. Below are the basic definitions and tools that will ease your entry into the stock market and make understanding financial information second nature.

Key Definitions

A company's *capital stock* represents the ownership of a corporation. Stock is divided into units, or *shares*, which each represent a fractional portion of the ownership. If a company has 2 million shares outstanding and you own 200 shares, for instance, you would own 1/10,000 of the company. Stock gives the owner the right to share in the net assets, net income, and management of the company.

The stock of a company is generally divided into two classes, *preferred* and *common. Preferred shares* have priority over common shares if a company is liquidated or if dividends are issued, which means they have more safety than common stocks, but they generally do not *appreciate* (rise in value) as much. That is because a preferred stock carries a fixed dividend rate and most have a *call price*, the price at which the company can redeem the issues at any time, so there is little incentive for an investor to pay a higher price. Preferred shares are favored by institutional investors looking for guranteed returns.

Most individuals, like us, invest in *common stocks*. They entitle their holders to a share in a company's assets and income. In addition, common shareholders exercise indirect control over the management of the company by electing board members. (Preferred shareholders generally do not have any voting rights.)

Income, if there is any, is shared with stockholders in the form of *dividends*. Dividends are issued at the discretion of the management, and are usually paid quarterly and in cash. (Well-run companies tend to issue dividends equal to no more than half the profits; the rest of the money is put back into the business.) In down periods, or periods of rapid growth, dividends for common stocks may be suspended or cut sharply.

The *stock market* in the United States includes three markets, or *exchanges*, where stocks are bought and sold: the New York Stock Exchange (NYSE), the largest and most prestigious; the American Stock Exchange (ASE); and the National Association of Securities Dealers Automatic Quotations (NASDAQ).

The owner of a share of stock can transfer that ownership by selling the stock to another buyer. Shares of stock are said to be *liquid* because they can be *traded*, which simply means bought and sold, almost instantaneously on the exchange where the company is listed. Investors make trades through a broker, who arranges these transactions for a fee (see Chapter 5).

When a company first issues stock for sale, in what is called an *initial public offering*, a price is set based on the estimated value of the company and market conditions. But once it is bought at that price, the stock can then be traded in the open market. There a company has only indirect influence over its price, by the manner in which it conducts business and by issuing additional shares (in an attempt to raise capital and broaden ownership) or by buying back shares (in an attempt to raise the price). Stock prices fluctuate depending on market reaction to events related to a company's business, such as the resignation of a key officer, the introduction of a promising new product, news events, or political and economic trends that may or may not be related to its business.

Investments in stocks are not insured by the federal government. So, in theory, if each company in which you invested was forced to liquidate its business, you could lose as much as you invested. On the other hand, if those companies grow and prosper, you may be rewarded with higher returns than those generated by more secure investments.

Calculating Gains and Losses

How do you know if you are winning or losing in the stock market? Your profit or loss from a stock is calculated by subtracting the price that you sold it for from the price that you bought it for.

Example: If you bought 100 shares of Wal-Mart for $35 a share and sold those shares later the same year for $70 a share, you would have a capital gain of $3,500, or a return of 100%. (Cost: 100 × $35 = $3,500. Sale price: 100 × $70 = $7,000. Profit: $7,000 − $3,500 = $3,500, or 100% of your original investment.)

Example: If you bought 100 shares of IBM for $200 a share and sold it later that year for $150 a share, you would have a loss of $500, or 25%. (Cost: 100 × $200 = $2,000. Sale price: 100 × $150 = $1,500. Loss: $1,500 − $2,000 = − $500, or 25% of your original investment)

Returns are trimmed by the fees you pay in commissions, because they add to the original cost of the stock. That's why it is important to watch how much you are spending in brokers' fees, especially if you are doing lots of trading.

Profits made from the sale of securities are taxed along with other forms of income. A *capital gains tax* is the amount levied on the difference between the cost of a capital asset and the sale price. Capital gains are taxed at a maximum rate of 28%. Capital losses may be used to lower taxable income, but some restrictions apply. We recommend consulting with a tax professional when figuring the taxes on your investment income. (For more information about club filing requirements, see p. 18.)

Basic Tools

The Wall Street Journal

The Wall Street Journal is our favorite source of daily business news. Its coverage is comprehensive and the front-page feature articles are reader-friendly. At least one member of your club should read it on a daily basis, looking for articles on stocks that you own or are considering for future purchase and sharing them with the group.

The *Journal* is also extremely useful because of its complete list of stock tables. As covering business news is a staple of most newspapers nowadays, you will probably find complete stock tables in your nearest big-city paper, too.

Stock Tables

52 Weeks		Stock	Sym	Div	Yld %	PE	Vol 100s	Hi	Lo	Close
Hi	Lo									
$27^1/_2$	$19^1/_2$	IBB Inc	IBB	.20	.8	15	128	$26^3/_2$	26	$26^1/_2$

Stock tables are published daily and summarize the previous day's trading activity. Monday's paper will list Friday's transactions; Tuesday's paper will list Monday's transactions; and so on.

There is a stock table for each of the three exchanges. Stocks are listed in alphabetical order based on a shortened version of the company name. If you cannot find the stock's abbreviation based on common sense (Wal-Mart, for example, is listed as WMT), you may have to call the company to ask how it is listed.

To the left of the abbreviation will be the high and low price the stock reached during the last year. The price is quoted in "points," with 1 point equal to one dollar and each eighth of a point equal to 12½ cents. For instance, if a stock's

52-week (or one year) high is 16⅞, the highest price it reached during the past year was $16.875.

Immediately to the right of the stock name is the dividend rate and percentage yield. The *dividend* is the current annual rate of dividend payment. The *yield* is the ratio of the annual dividend to the closing price. We tend to ignore these because we are looking for growth in a company's stock price rather than income from dividends. Often, companies that issue high dividends have a steady income stream but little prospects for rapid growth.

The third column to the right lists each stock's *p/e ratio*, a calculation that divides stock price by annual earnings per share. A stock's p/e ratio gives you an indication of the value of a stock. It is a way to compare stocks and to compare the current performance of a stock with its past performance. Generally, the lower the p/e ratio, the better. However, you should also compare a company's current p/e ratio with its ratios over the past five years. If the current ratio is lower than the five-year average ratio, you may have spotted a good buy.

Example: If Stock A was selling for $2 a share and its annual earnings per share were .50, its p/e ratio would be 4. If Stock B was selling for only $1 a share but its earnings per share were .10, its p/e ratio would be 10. Based on an examination of p/e ratio, Stock A would be a better buy than Stock B.

The last four columns are the ones that we get excited about. First comes the high price that the stock reached during the entire day of trading. The next column lists the low for the day. The third column, marked "last," lists the stock's last, or closing, price for the day. Closing prices are used in calculating gains or losses between particular periods of time. The final column, marked "chg," gives the amount that the closing price changed compared to the closing price the day before. A plus sign indicates a rise in price;

a minus sign indicates a drop. For example, $^+\frac{1}{2}$ means that the closing price of the stock was $.50 higher than the closing price of the day before.

> **Remember: You can track the activity of a stock on a daily basis by looking up its closing price in the stock tables. But profits or losses are not realized until you actually sell a stock.**

Value Line and Annual Reports

Value Line's Investment Survey and the annual reports issued by public companies are required reading for the serious investor. In their annual reports, companies summarize their activities during the past year and discuss their plans for the future. Annual reports also include balance sheets and income statements, key sources of financial information.

Value Line's Investment Survey provides analysis of the information contained in the annual report. *Value Line* analysts apply their knowledge of the economy, industries, and individual companies to analyze each company's financial history, current health, and future prospects. It's a gold mine of useful information.

These tools are so important, in fact, that they merit their own chapters. Read on!

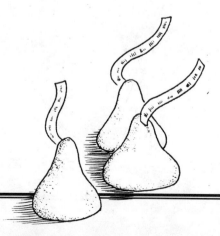

10. Mining Gold from *Value Line's Investment Survey*

Value *Line's Investment Survey* is surely one of the most useful tools available to the investor. "It's the next best thing to having your own private securities analyst," says Peter Lynch. Available in most large public libraries and subscribed to by nearly all brokerage houses, *Value Line* neatly crams just about everything you need to know about a publicly traded company onto one side of a letter-sized sheet.

Each page follows the same format, so once you familiarize yourself with one write-up, you can easily research any of the more than 1,700 companies indexed in the survey. In the center of the page (see *Value Line* sample, p. 82) is a

Value Line Sheet: Rubbermaid

RUBBERMAID NYSE-RBD	RECENT PRICE 26	P/E RATIO 18.3 (Trailing: 19.7 Median: 22.0)	RELATIVE P/E RATIO 1.19	DIV'D YLD 1.7%	VALUE LINE 969

TIMELINESS	3 Average (Relative Price Performance Next 12 Mos.)
SAFETY	2 Above Average (Scale: 1 Highest to 5 Lowest)
BETA	1.25 (1.00 = Market)

1997-99 PROJECTIONS

	Price	Gain	Ann'l Total Return
High	55	(+110%)	22%
Low	45	(+75%)	16%

Insider Decisions

	J	A	S	O	N	D	J	F	M
to Buy	0	0	0	0	1	0	0	0	0
Options	0	0	0	0	0	0	0	0	0
to Sell	1	2	1	0	2	0	0	0	1

Institutional Decisions

	2Q93	3Q93	4Q93
to Buy	106	111	95
to Sell	121	118	110
Hld's(000)	70302	73217	74170

Target Price Range 1997 1998 1999

Relative Price Strength

Percent shares traded 4.5 / 3.0 / 1.5

Shaded areas indicate recessions

Options: PACE

© VALUE LINE PUB., INC. 97-99

1978	1979	1980	1981	1982	1983	1984	1985	1986	1987	1988	1989	1990	1991	1992	1993	1994	1995			© VALUE LINE PUB., INC.	97-99
2.09	2.48	2.72	2.89	3.04	3.52	4.19	4.63	5.43	6.91	8.12	9.12	9.59	10.41	11.27	12.22	13.20	14.45			Sales per sh	18.65
.24	.28	.24	.33	.36	.43	.50	.60	.71	.90	1.00	1.22	1.24	1.41	1.58	1.82	2.00	2.25			"Cash Flow" per sh	3.30
.15	.19	.12	.21	.22	.29	.35	.40	.48	.58	.68	.79	.90	1.02	1.15	1.32	1.45	1.65			Earnings per sh A	2.50
.05	.05	.06	.07	.08	.09	.10	.11	.13	.16	.19	.23	.27	.31	.35	.41	.47	.55			Div'ds Decl'd per sh B ■	.75
.17	.30	.28	.17	.13	.16	.34	.47	.47	.69	.57	.58	.65	.76	.84	.98	.35	.80			Cap'l Spending per sh	.80
.94	1.07	1.12	1.25	1.39	1.59	1.77	2.08	2.45	2.97	3.48	4.06	4.80	5.53	6.16	7.05	8.00	9.05			Book Value per sh C	13.65
123.74	123.07	123.21	123.58	123.83	124.03	135.29	144.95	146.50	146.86	147.00	147.33	159.99	160.19	160.24	160.36	160.50	161.00			Common Shs Outst'g D	161.00
11.2	8.6	13.7	9.8	12.2	18.1	13.9	16.7	23.1	24.2	17.7	19.8	20.7	26.0	27.8	24.4	Bold figures are				Avg Ann'l P/E Ratio	20.0
1.53	1.24	1.82	1.19	1.34	1.53	1.29	1.36	1.57	1.62	1.47	1.50	1.54	1.66	1.69	1.44	Value Line estimates				Relative P/E Ratio	1.55
2.6%	3.3%	3.8%	3.3%	2.9%	1.7%	2.0%	1.7%	1.2%	1.1%	1.6%	1.5%	1.4%	1.2%	1.1%	1.3%					Avg Ann'l Div'd Yield	1.5%

CAPITAL STRUCTURE as of 12/31/93

Total Debt $34.9 mill. Due in 5 Yrs $26.6 mill.
LT Debt $19.4 mill. LT Interest $1.5 mill.

(Total interest coverage: 44.9x) (2% of Cap'l)

Pension Liability None

Pfd Stock None

Common Stock 160,357,086 shs. (98% of Cap'l)

																				© VALUE LINE PUB., INC.	97-99
566.4	671.4	795.2	1015.0	1193.5	1343.9	1534.0	1667.3	1805.3	1960.2	2115	2325			Sales ($mill)	3000
19.0%	21.0%	21.2%	20.4%	18.3%	19.7%	18.8%	19.2%	20.2%	21.8%	22.5%	23.0%			Operating Margin	26.5%
21.1	30.3	33.3	47.5	47.4	62.7	55.4	62.7	69.9	80.9	90.0	100			Depreciation ($mill)	130
46.9	57.1	70.1	84.5	99.3	116.4	143.5	162.7	184.0	211.4	230	265			Net Profit ($mill)	405
45.6%	46.7%	47.7%	42.9%	37.8%	38.9%	37.9%	38.1%	37.5%	38.2%	39.0%	39.0%			Income Tax Rate	39.0%
8.3%	8.5%	8.8%	8.3%	8.3%	8.7%	9.4%	9.8%	10.2%	10.8%	10.9%	11.4%			Net Profit Margin	13.5%
127.2	152.3	153.3	181.1	221.5	313.3	367.4	418.5	476.4	570.4	675	830			Working Cap'l ($mill)	1550
21.9	33.1	35.7	40.0	39.0	50.3	39.2	27.8	20.3	19.4	20.0	20.0			Long-Term Debt ($mill)	200
239.0	301.7	359.4	435.9	511.4	598.4	768.2	885.7	987.6	1130.5	1285	1460			Net Worth ($mill)	2200
18.3%	17.5%	18.2%	18.1%	18.4%	18.3%	18.2%	18.0%	18.4%	18.5%	17.5%	18.0%			% Earned Total Cap'l	18.5%
19.6%	18.9%	19.5%	19.4%	19.4%	19.5%	18.7%	18.4%	18.6%	18.7%	18.0%	18.0%			% Earned Net Worth	18.5%

High: 6.3 / 5.7 / 8.7 / 14.3 / 17.5 / 13.5 / 18.9 / 22.5 / 38.3 / 37.3 / 37.4 / 35.8
Low: 3.7 / 4.1 / 5.5 / 8.3 / 9.5 / 10.5 / 12.5 / 15.5 / 18.5 / 27.0 / 27.6 / 25.9

2-for-1 split (multiple)

15.5 x "Cash Flow" p sh

CURRENT POSITION ($MILL.)	1991	1992	12/31/93
Cash Assets	153.3	122.5	194.1
Receivables	277.0	295.0	322.3
Inventory (LIFO)	225.2	271.9	303.4
Other	8.5	10.2	9.9
Current Assets	664.0	699.6	829.7
Accts Payable	117.8	99.6	116.4
Debt Due	26.4	23.7	15.5
Other	101.3	99.9	127.4
Current Liab.	245.5	223.2	259.3

ANNUAL RATES of change (per sh)	Past 10 Yrs.	Past 5 Yrs.	Est'd '91-'93 to '97-'99
Sales	13.5%	10.5%	8.5%
"Cash Flow"	15.5%	13.0%	13.0%
Earnings	17.0%	15.0%	14.0%
Dividends	16.5%	17.5%	13.0%
Book Value	16.0%	16.0%	14.0%

QUARTERLY SALES ($ mill.)					
Cal-endar	Mar.31	Jun.30	Sep.30	Dec.31	Full Year
1991	410.9	417.3	429.4	409.7	1667.3
1992	448.4	449.1	473.5	434.3	1805.3
1993	483.7	488.5	515.2	472.9	1960.2
1994	491.6	550	555	518.4	2115
1995	570	585	610	560	2325

EARNINGS PER SHARE A					
Cal-endar	Mar.31	Jun.30	Sep.30	Dec.31	Full Year
1991	.24	.25	.29	.24	1.02
1992	.27	.27	.33	.28	1.15
1993	.31	.32	.37	.32	1.32
1994	.32	.36	.42	.35	1.45
1995	.35	.40	.48	.42	1.65

QUARTERLY DIVIDENDS PAID B■					
Cal-endar	Mar.31	Jun.30	Sep.30	Dec.31	Full Year
1990	.065	.065	.065	.075	.27
1991	.075	.075	.075	.085	.31
1992	.085	.085	.085	.0975	.35
1993	.0975	.0975	.0975	.1125	.35
1994	.1125				.41

(A) Based on avg. shares outstanding. Next egs. report due late Jul. Includes gain (losses) from discontinued operations: '77, 3¢; '79, (4¢); '80, (19¢). Excl. nonrecur. gains (losses): '92. (13¢). (B) Next dividend meeting about Jul. 15. Goes ex about May 10. Dividend payment dates: Mar. 1, June 3, Sept. 3, Dec. 2. ■ Div'd reinvestment plan available. (C) Incl. in- tangibles. In '93: $111.2 mill., 70¢/sh. (D) In millions, adjusted for stock splits.

BUSINESS: Rubbermaid Inc. makes plastic and rubber products. Products include kitchenware, laundry & bath accessories, microwave ovenware, patio furniture, ready-to-assemble household furniture, products for home horticulture, office, food service, health care, and industrial maintenance. Acquired *Little Tikes* children's toys, '84; Microcomputer Accessories and Seco Inds. floor care products, '88. Eldon Industries (office supplies, soldering tools), '91. Foreign operations, 11% of sales; Research & development, 1.4%. 1993 depreciation rate: 7.5%. Has about 11,978 employees, 22,508 shareholders. Chairman and Chief Executive Officer: Wolfgang R. Schmitt. Incorporated: Ohio. Address: 1147 Akron Road, Wooster, Ohio 44691. Telephone: 216-264-6464.

It's been a tough winter for Rubbermaid. The company experienced operational difficulties due to the severe weather conditions. And retail customers opted not to shop as often as usual, so final sell-through wasn't impressive. **The company also had to deal with some structural issues.** For several years now, the retail sector has been consolidating and learning to get by with increasingly lean inventories. This puts a lot of pressure on manufacturers, who are forced to cope with smaller order sizes and shorter lead times. There's a limit as to how lean retail stocks can get, and we think the adjustment process is near its end, but that stage hasn't yet been reached. **But we expect Rubbermaid to log a healthy full-year earnings gain.** In recent weeks, as the weather improved, business picked up. And Rubbermaid is continuing its long-standing efforts to enhance its productivity. We're also encouraged by the fact that Rubbermaid's *Little Tikes* line (which focuses on non fad toys) was well received at the latest trade show. Too, the company is launching some new marketing initiatives. For example,

Little Tikes will be very conspicuous in the new Toys R Us catalog. And Rubbermaid will utilize advertising inserts in home magazines. Also . . . **Rubbermaid's new product effort is in full swing.** The company has a goal of having 35% of annual sales come from products introduced in the past five years, and entering a new field every 12 to 18 months. Some of these new products are quite novel, such as ready-to-assemble furniture (which is easier to assemble than traditional wood products), resin wheelbarrows, tractor carts, and office furniture. But in other cases, the offerings can be quite subtle, such as reintroducing an old product with a new look. Indeed, the finding of new ways to utilize resin technology has, we believe, been the single biggest factor behind Rubbermaid's impressive historical growth. **This stock usually commands a high P/E multiple,** making it very responsive to shifts in investor sentiment. The stock's recent softness, in response to the pending flattish first quarter, may present a good 3- to 5-year buying opportunity.

Marc H. Gerstein   April 22, 1994

Company's Financial Strength	A+
Stock's Price Stability	70
Price Growth Persistence	95
Earnings Predictability	100

To subscribe call 1-800-833-0046.

concise summary of the company's major product lines, recent acquisitions, and other key information such as percentage of sales accounted for by foreign operations, portion of revenues spent on research and development, or number of employees. The name of the chief executive officer and the address and telephone number of corporate headquarters are also included.

Below the company description are several insightful paragraphs about the firm's prospects, signed by a *Value Line* analyst. In the page devoted to Rubbermaid, for instance, the writer explains why its shares tend to be more volatile than its earnings predictability might warrant. ("At times, investors become so enamored with Rubbermaid's corporate prowess that they bid the stock up to levels that cannot be justified.... Once Wall Street recognizes that this has occurred, corrections take place.")

The rest of each sheet is jam-packed with figures. From *Value Line's* charts, you can get a bird's-eye view of a company's performance for the past 15 years and its projected performance for the next two or three. You can quickly see if a company has had a steady rate of increases in its earnings per share, sales, and profits in the past, and if increases are projected in the future.

From a small box labeled "Capital Structure," you can calculate a company's debt as a portion of its assets. Another box lists the quarterly dividends paid over the last five years. Have they been paid with regularity? Has the amount increased over time? (We don't worry about the dividend, but for Rubbermaid, the answer to both questions is yes.) You can also find a company's price-earnings ratio, beta, and projections (both a high and low) for its stock price over the next three years.

Value Line also calculates a company's ranking on several of its own scales. The first is "timeliness," which is a measure of its expected price performance over the next year. The second is "safety," a measure of the volatility of its stock price. In both scales 1 is the highest rating; 2 is above average; 3 is average; 4 is below average; and 5 is lowest.

Finally, in the bottom right-hand corner, *Value Line* grades a company's financial strength (from A^{++} all the way down to C); its stock's price stability (a scale of 100 to NMF*); its price growth persistence (100 to NMF*); and earnings predictability (100 to NMF*).

As you review a company's write-up, if anything jumps out at you that is not what you are looking for, do like Ann says: Turn the page and read another one.

* NMF: No Mentionable Figure.

11. How to Scrutinize an Annual Report

Public companies attempt to put the best face on their performance every 12 months in a yearly ritual known as the annual report, a magazine-length, slickly produced booklet that is distributed to shareholders, the media, and interested members of the public. Though annual reports are largely public relations efforts, Securities and Exchange Commission (SEC) regulations require that they also contain some standard financial information. The company's description of its operations and strategies in the text and the numbers in the financial charts can give you some insight into a company.

Annual reports are automatically sent to shareholders

and will be sent on request to anyone else. They are typically issued about three months after a company's fiscal year ends. If a company's fiscal year closed in December, for example, its 1993 annual report would be available in March 1994.

Most annual reports open with a letter to shareholders from the chief executive officer of the company. The CEO generally reviews the past year, citing highlights, explaining difficulties, and laying out the plans for the next year or more. If a company had a difficult year, see if the CEO uses candor in the letter and thoughtfully explains his or her strategy for the future. If, on the other hand, past problems are glossed over without any significant insight into reversing them, you may have cause for concern.

Warren Buffett, one of the country's most successful investors, is known for being unusually straightforward in his letters to shareholders of Berkshire Hathaway, the diversified company he presides over as chairman and CEO. Here is a sample from the 1976 annual report:

> Our textile division was a significant disappointment during 1976. Earnings, measured either by return on sales or by return on capital employed, were inadequate. In part, this was due to industry conditions which did not measure up to expectations of a year ago. But equally important were our own shortcomings. Marketing efforts and mill capabilities were not properly matched in our new Waumbec operation. Unfavorable manufacturing cost variances were produced by improper evaluation of machinery and personnel capabilities.

Most CEOs are not so frank, but if they come even close to Buffett, that is a good sign.

The rest of the text will most likely discuss the company's operations in general terms, highlighting major accomplishments—discoveries, new products, acquisitions, and the like. From this, you can discern what aspects of its business the company regards as most important.

More significant to outsiders, however, are the financial charts, which tell a more objective story. (These figures are generally audited by a reputable accounting firm. Make sure to read the auditor's opinion, which should include a routine endorsement of the figures, stating that they are "presented fairly . . . in conformity with generally accepted accounting principles." If there is a more qualified endorsement, read it closely because it may signal a problem.)

Balance Sheet

The *balance sheet,* the first page of numbers that you should examine closely, is a snapshot of the company's financial condition at year end. The balance sheet juxtaposes three key sets of figures: assets, liabilities, and shareholders' equity. *Assets* are things of value owned by the company, including inventories and property, plant, and equipment. *Liabilities* are claims against the firm, including long-term debt and taxes. *Shareholders' equity* is the value of the stockholders' share of the business, which is the excess of assets over liabilities. In other words, the assets always equal—or balance—liabilities plus shareholders' equity.

Current assets are items that are expected to be converted into cash within a year. They are listed in order of their ease of convertibility to cash, starting with *cash* itself and including items like accounts receivable and inventories. *Accounts receivable* indicates the amount due from customers for goods already sold, minus an allowance for nonpayment by "doubtful accounts." *Inventories* include unsold finished goods, work in progress, and raw materials. Since they will not be converted into cash until the goods are sold, inventories are nearer to the end of the list.

Fixed assets are *property*, *plant*, and *equipment*, valuable resources that the company does not plan to convert into cash within a year. They may include buildings, office equipment, machinery, and delivery trucks. Because fixed assets, except for land, will wear out and lose their value over time, companies allow for depreciation. For instance, if a fleet of trucks was bought for $500,000 and is expected to serve the company for five years, $100,000, or one-fifth of the cost, will be added to the depreciation account each year. At the end of five years, the cost will have been accounted for. (Some companies use an accelerated depreciation plan that permits greater deductions in earlier years.) The *net property*, *plant*, and *equipment* figure reflects the fixed assets minus depreciation.

> **Current assets plus net property, plant, and equipment equal total assets.**

Current liabilities are debts that are due within a year. *Accounts payable* are debts owed to creditors for items such as materials, supplies, and services. Also included under current liabilities are *current maturities of long-term debt*, which are debts to lenders that are due within a year, *lease obligations*, and *income taxes*.

Long-term debt includes bonds and other debt secured by company property.

> **Current liabilities plus long-term debt equal total liabilities.**

Shareholders' equity indicates how many shares of *preferred* and *common* stock are outstanding. Preferred shares are listed first because they have a prior claim before common shareholders to dividends and assets. Should a company go out of business, common shareholders will be paid only after all bondholders and preferred shareholders are compensated.

Retained earnings indicate the amount that the company reserved for the growth of the business before paying dividends to shareholders.

Analyzing the Balance Sheet

Now that you know the key terms, it is time to analyze the balance sheet. The first thing to do is to subtract current liabilities from current assets to derive a measure of *working capital*. Does the company have an amount that is sufficient to permit it to continue operations even if business falls off for an extended period?

A second key indicator is the *current ratio*, which you can determine by dividing current assets by current liabilities. A 2-to-1 ratio is acceptable for manufacturing companies. A ratio of less than 2 to 1 is a danger sign, because the company could run short of working capital to meet short-term cash requirements. (Utilities are an exception; they can operate successfully with ratios of 1 to 1 or less.) If the ratio is lower than that for past years or less than its competitors, the company may be at a disadvantage.

An even more telling ratio is the so-called *acid test*, which divides current assets excluding inventories by current liabilities. Because inventories are not easily converted into cash, this is a more realistic way to evaluate a company's ability to cover current debts. If inventories are too large a portion of assets, it may signal a cash flow problem or the presence of a large amount of undesirable merchandise.

Manic Manufacturing Company

CURRENT ASSETS

Cash	$4,500,000
Accounts Receivable-Less Allowance for doubtful assets	6,750,000
Inventories	22,500,000
Total Current Assets	$33,750,000

PROPERTY, PLANT AND EQUIPMENT

Cost	$40,000,000	
Accumulated Depreciation	7,300,000	
Net Property		32,700,000
Total Assets		$66,450,000

Balance Sheet — December 31, 199X

CURRENT LIABILITIES

Accounts Payable	$3,000,000
Accrued taxes	2,000,000
Accrued wages, interest, and other Expense	1,225,000
Total Current Liabilities	$6,225,000

LONG-TERM DEBT

Mortgage bonds	$12,000,000	
Debentures	6,000,000	
Total Long-Term Debt		$18,000,000

SHAREHOLDERS' EQUITY

Preferred Stock, 100,000 shares		
$100 Par Value		10,000,000
Common stock,	6,750,000 shares	
No Par value		20,000,000
Amounts Contributed above Stated Value		
(arising from sale of stock)		$7,000,000
Retained earnings		5,225,000
Total Shareholders' Equity		$42,225,000
Total Liabilities and Shareholders' Equity		$66,450,000

Income Statement

Now turn to the *income statement*, which measures a company's profitability over time. At the top of the statement is the figure for *net sales*, the amount of money collected for all goods or services sold minus returns and allowances. Underneath net sales will be a list of the *operating costs and expenses*, which may include cost of goods sold, marketing and administrative expenses, research and development, and other expenses. Subtract operating costs and expenses from net sales and the result will be *operating income*. To calculate *net income* (also known as the "bottom line" because it falls at the bottom of the chart), operating income is added to *other income* minus *taxes*. The bottom line is important to shareholders because that is the source of dividend payments.

To measure *inventory turnover*, divide the *cost of goods sold* by the total inventory figure on the balance sheet. If the cost of goods sold is $500,000 and the inventory is $100,000, the inventory turnover is five times. Generally, the higher the turnover the better, but you should compare this figure with those of competitors because norms vary by industry.

Plant turnover is another useful ratio: sales divided by property, plant, and equipment. Again, the higher the better, and it should increase over time. If a company increases its expenditures without growing sales, assets are probably not being used efficiently.

Using numbers from the income statement, you can calculate the *profit margin*, a figure that means little on its own, but that you want to rise over a period of years. Divide "profit before taxes" by "net sales." If the profit margin is rising, management may be cutting costs successfully. The text may give you clues as to whether the company plans further cost reductions, which is good for profitability.

Manic Manufacturing Company Income Statement
For the year ending December 31, 199X

Net Sales	$67,500,000
Cost of Sales	45,000,000
Gross Profit	$22,500,000
Selling, general and administrative expenses	$15,000,000
Operating Profit	7,500,000
Other Income	$900,000
	$8,400,000
Other Expenses	945,000
Net Income Before Taxes	$7,455,000
Provisions For Federal Income Taxes	3,877,500
Net Income After Taxes	$3,577,500

Return on equity can be figured by consulting both the income statement and the balance sheet. This is determined by dividing net income by *book value*. Book value is the "value of common stock" plus "retained earnings" plus "surplus reserves," all figures which can be found on the balance sheet.

Finally, you may want to calculate *sales per employee*. Simply divide net sales by the number of employees, another figure that you would like to see rise over time. With both "return on equity" and "sales per employee," the higher the ratio the better. Even more important, however, is growth over time and better performance than competitors.

Don't worry if at first you feel slightly overwhelmed by all the figuring. Like return on equity in a well-managed company, your understanding will grow over time.

Investing

12. Investing On Your Own: Using Lessons from the Club for Personal Investing

You can use the Beardstown Ladies' method to invest on your own. The same strategies for evaluating, picking, and selling stocks work as well for an individual portfolio as for that of a club.

It is quite common to build an individual portfolio at the same time you are contributing to an investment club. Retirees who are seeking additional capital or couples with a specific short-term goal, such as raising money for a down payment on a house, often employ such a strategy. As individuals, they may invest in the market with a specific goal in mind and then sell some or all of their stock when they reach that goal. (If you are trying to save a specific amount, remember that once you sell your securities, you will have to pay a tax on your profits, which are called *capital gains*. Capital gains are taxed like other income, but the maximum rate of taxation is 28%.) As members of a club, they continue to hone their investment skills and expand their knowledge about different companies.

Many people use their membership in an investment club as a bellwether for their personal investments. Some apply the club's strategy—buying growth stocks with the intention of holding them as a long-term investment. Others buy some or all of the stocks in their club's portfolio.

We also have partners who limit their ownership of individual stocks to what they buy with the club, supplementing their club accounts with individual investments in mutual funds, Treasury bonds, CDs, savings accounts, and annuities.

Club membership can be valuable to all types of investors since it provides a kind of continuing education course on investing. Because economic conditions, tax laws, corporate news, and investment vehicles are always changing, it's hard for even the most experienced amateur investor to keep up! For less-experienced stock pickers, club membership is a way to build confidence if you desire to invest on your own. In fact, many of our partners who felt ill at ease buying stock on their own when they first joined the club, began to put together their own portfolio, either on their own or with the help of a broker or financial planner, after a few years.

Pay Yourself First

This is so important! Whether you plan to build your own portfolio, supplement your investments in a club, or just study the market for a while, don't let a month pass without investing in yourself. Each month, set aside your bills until you determine how much you can save. Pay yourself before you pay anyone else. It doesn't matter if it's only $5 or $10 to start, as long as you put something aside for savings on a regular basis.

If your expenses exceed your income, then go over your budget carefully and cut out whatever you can to make room for some monthly savings. How about giving up a meal out or a couple of new compact discs every month? It won't be long before you realize the benefits of your sacrifice as you watch your savings grow. (As soon as you feel you can increase the amount you are saving, you should.)

"Each month I put away a certain amount of money in savings and that is my money," explains Lillian Ellis. "I do that on top of everything else, even before I pay a bill. If more people would use that formula, I think they would get along a lot better. I found out it works for me." If you attempt to save money the other way—waiting to set aside money until *after* you pay your creditors—it's almost guaranteed that there won't be anything left over for you. (We don't know why, it just seems to be part of the human condition.)

Paying dues to an investment club is one way of paying yourself first, because you set aside $25 (or whatever the club's monthly dues are) each month for investment purposes. But if you can add more to your savings regularly outside the club, by all means do.

If you are building a portfolio on your own, membership in an investment club can also provide you with useful research. You will learn about many more industries and companies than you would have time to study on your own. By splitting the work with fellow investors, club members learn far more from a few hours of participation in the group than in hours spent in solitary research at the library (and it's more fun).

If a partner learns about a promising enterprise, it is not unusual for her to call a broker the next morning and make a personal investment in that stock. In the case of Aunt

Margaret, she bought Kellogg's, a stock that the club had studied but decided *against* investing in. After she sold the stock some months later, she showed off her investment savvy by driving around in the new car she bought with the profits.

NAIC Investment Guidelines

NAIC advocates the following investment principles:

1. INVEST a set sum once a month in common stocks, regardless of general market conditions;
2. REINVEST DIVIDENDS and capital gains immediately;
3. BUY GROWTH STOCKS—companies whose sales are increasing at a rate faster than their industry in general, and that have good prospects for continued growth; and
4. INVEST IN DIFFERENT FIELDS. Diversification helps spread risk and opportunity.

13. How to Pick Stocks: The Beardstown Ladies' Method

Fundamentals vs. Market Timing: How We Stay Calm When Everyone Else Panics

Experienced stock pickers generally choose one of two popular methods for investing: they rely either on *fundamentals* or *market timing*. Call us fundamentalists.

Investing in fundamentals means looking for value inherent in a company and seeking a profit by holding on to its stock while that value grows. Fundamentalists—like us—are generally conservative investors with a long-term outlook. We expect stock prices to rise as value grows. We are fascinated with the quality of individual companies. And pay little attention to the daily gyrations of the market.

Market timers, in contrast, scrutinize the ups and downs in the market and the price trends of particular stocks. They focus on market indicators, such as the Dow Jones Industrial Average (an index of 30 major stocks traded on the New York Stock Exchange), and attempt to capitalize on day-to-day fluctuations in stock prices.

When you invest based on a company's fundamentals, if its price drops, you rarely think of bailing out. Instead, we view it as an opportunity to buy more stock at a bargain price!

Ignoring the daily fluctuations of the market is part of the creed of fundamentalists. We admit that it is not always easy, but in down markets many of the most experienced and successful investors are the only ones left, using the opportunity to buy more stocks. When inexperienced investors rush back in later as prices start to climb again, the experienced investors score some of their biggest gains. Have faith and remember: *Even with all the drops, over the last century the market's general direction has been up!*

For the last decade, the S&P 500, the index of 500 stocks that represent the major industry sectors and all the large companies traded on the New York Stock Exchange, has grown an average of 11% each year; not a bad return. If you had invested in all 500 stocks in the index, you would have replicated the market's performance. We aim higher. Our goal is earning an annual return of 14.7%, which means doubling our money every five years and beating the market consistently.

Success depends largely on doing our homework and being selective. We can't stress this enough: You simply cannot make good investment decisions on the spur of the moment, based on intuition or "hot tips" from friends and relatives. Each stock should be carefully studied and evaluated *before* it is purchased.

10 Basic Ingredients to Choosing Profitable Stocks

No stock-picking method can guarantee profitable returns all the time, but if you consistently follow our basic guidelines when you evaluate stocks, you will increase your chance of selecting solid growth stocks to bolster your bottom line.

Consider these 10 ingredients when you look at a potential investment. These, combined with a large dose of common sense, add up to our recipe for successful stock picking:

1. **Industry ranking.** The first thing to investigate is a company's industry ranking in *Value Line's Investment Survey. Value Line* is an invaluable investment tool (see Chapter 10, Mining Gold from *Value Line's Investment Survey*) that can be found in most local libraries and some banks.

    Restrict your holdings to stocks that *Value Line* ranks in the top third of their industry, preferably among the top 25.

2. **Timeliness.** *Value Line* ranks stocks between 1 and 5 for "timeliness," a prediction of "relative price performance for the next 12 months"—in other words, how fast its price will grow relative to other stocks. Limit your candidates to stocks that have a *Value Line* timeliness rating of 1 (highest) or 2 (above average).

3. **Safety.** All stocks carry risk, but it is possible to calculate their relative risk. We depend on *Value Line*'s safety rating for each stock we are

considering. Safety, as measured by *Value Line,* is the volatility of a stock's price around its own long-term trend. The narrower the band of fluctuation, the lower the rating and the safer the stock. The wider the band, the less safe, or more risky. Choose stocks that have a rating of 1 (highest) or 2 (above average).

4. **Debt.** Select companies whose total debt is equal to no more than a third of total assets. In our judgment, the lower the debt, the better the investment. Debt and asset figures can be found in *Value Line,* in *Standard & Poor's Stock Reports* (also widely available in libraries), or in a company's annual report.

5. **Beta.** A beta is a number that compares the volatility (movement) of a stock's price relative to that of the total market. A beta of 1 means that a stock price moves up and down at the same rate as the market as a whole. A beta of 2 means that when the market drops or rises 10%, the stock price is likely to move double that, or 20%.

Here again, we consult *Value Line* or *Standard & Poor's* for this number. Prime candidates for investment for us are stocks that have a beta between .90 and 1.10 because they are not much more or less volatile than the whole market.

6. **Sales and earnings.** We look for companies that have at least five years of solid growth in sales and earnings. Then we evaluate each company's potential for future growth: Is its industry growing? Does the company itself have good growth potential? Will that growth be passed on to the shareholders?

We select companies whose sales and earnings are expected to grow by double digits in the next few years. The sales of a small company should be projected to grow 12% to 15% or even higher; a medium-sized company should grow 10% to 12%; for a large established company, 7% to 10% growth is a good rate. To calculate this, refer to *Value Line*'s earnings projections.

7. **Stock price.** Early in a club's history, you might try to buy stocks that cost less than $25 per share. The cheaper the price, the easier it is to buy an even lot (100 shares at a time), which minimizes brokers' fees.

Of course, you may make exceptions when a stock at a higher price is still a good value. We bought 25 shares of Quaker Oats at $72.74, for instance, because we liked what we were reading and hearing about the stock. We later sold stock in two companies to buy another 75 shares to make an even block of 100.

8. **Price-earnings ratio.** The price-earnings ratio, the price of a security divided by earnings per share, determines the cost of a stock relative to its projected earnings. We track the price-earnings ratio for the last five years and restrict our investments to companies that have a p/e ratio at or below the average for that period. P/e ratios are listed in stock tables found in daily newspapers. *Value Line* lists average annual p/e ratios going back 15 years.

9. **Upside-down ratio.** You can identify stocks whose prices are more likely to rise than fall by calculating their "upside-down ratio," which evaluates the relative odds of potential gain versus the risk of loss for a given price per share. A 3-to-1 potential upside in the projected appreciation of the stock is preferred. You can find projected highs

and lows listed in (where else?) *Value Line,* whose analysts develop estimates based on their knowledge of each company and their predictions for industry and economic growth.

> **Example: Determine the projected high price ($40). Subtract the present cost ($15). This leaves you with $25. Take the present cost ($15) and subtract the projected low ($10). This leaves you with $5. Divide the $25 (upside potential) by $5 (downside risk). This gives you a ratio of 5:1, a good buy.**

10. **Management.** Even with all the right numbers, a company can be a poor investment if the wrong managers take the helm. Try to invest in companies that are run by people with solid track records. You can evaluate management's performance by studying articles in the business press, *Value Line*'s text about the company, analysts' reports (available from your broker), and materials and presentations prepared by the company officials themselves. Company officials should be in control of any outstanding problems and engaged in adequate planning for the future.

> **Example: We bought 50 shares of Wolverine Worldwide at $12.48 (including commission) in 1992 because it seemed like ladies were wearing more sensible shoes to work, and, because Wolverine makes footwear that is popular with farmers, we knew they had good products.**

Later they were involved in a lawsuit over the quality of their pigskin and their price fell to half what we paid.

Betty Sinnock heard the company's management make a presentation at an NAIC conference in Orlando in November 1992. They had settled the lawsuit and said they were selling off a line of athletic shoes that had been a losing venture. The Wolverine officials felt that 1993 was going to be a very good year for them, with a growth of earnings in the 14% range. She shared this information with the club at the next meeting and we voted to buy an additional 150 shares. The stock has since climbed as high as 35.

Optional ingredient: Personal preferences.

We do not have a club policy against investing in any type of stock, but there are some areas we are content to avoid. We have not invested in the stocks of tobacco or liquor manufacturers or in companies that make money from gambling. We also pay some attention to how companies treat their employees—we think poor treatment often negatively affects the bottom line. When CIPSCO, the local utility, locked out its employees, for instance, we felt inclined to sell our stock. We decided to do so, and consequently got out before the price took a nose dive.

We also avoid initial public offerings, stocks that are offered to the public for the first time—again, not by policy, but because we prefer to invest based on a record of several years of earnings growth as a public company.

Finding Companies to Research

Once you begin looking for stocks in which to invest, you will discover many valuable sources at your fingertips. A trip to the library, careful reading of your local newspapers, and discussions with your neighbors as well as professional brokers can all give you leads worth investigating. These are our primary sources for "hot tips":

1. *Business publications* are a very fertile source of investment leads. We comb articles for information about trends, new products, and economic news that may affect particular industries or companies. *The Wall Street Journal* is the preeminent source of daily business news in the country. Assign a member to follow the stocks in your portfolio by scanning the *Journal* index each day (it is published Monday through Friday) and clipping articles about companies in which the club has invested. In between meetings she should send relevant clips to the club member who is following that particular stock.

   Other informative publications include *Fortune, Forbes, Kiplinger's Personal Finance Magazine,* and *BusinessWeek.*

2. Value Line's *List of Timely Industries* also will give you many good ideas. Choose an industry from that list and then pick three promising companies to research.

3. *Better Investing,* NAIC's monthly magazine, provides several suggestions of stocks to study in every issue.

4. *Company materials and representatives.* You can also learn about companies directly from their representatives who attend regional investment fairs

and NAIC conventions. If you have a question about a company or want printed material, do not hesitate to call the company's investor relations department. Usually they will be happy to help.

5. *Your broker*, who is a professional investor, can be a good source as well. Our broker, Homer Rieken, first told us about VeriFone, for instance, which we bought in 1991. But we never follow his advice without first doing our own evaluation of a stock. (The price fell after we bought it, but we couldn't blame Homer because the final decision was ours. Since we had done our research, we didn't panic because we felt its fundamentals were strong and that it was a promising company.)

6. *Life experiences and common sense.* Keep your eyes open for promising companies and industries. We first became interested in Wal-Mart, for example, when the company opened a store in Beardstown. Concern about environmental issues prompted our investment in Waste Management, a large firm that has a contract to remove waste in our town.

Doing the Research: The Stock Selection Committee

The Stock Selection Committee, which does the initial research on potential investments, is the heart of any investment club. The committee should be made up of two or three volunteers who serve until a transaction—a buy or sell order—is executed. Typically, each member serves on the committee about once a year. A committee's term may last only one month or over a period of several months and adds a few extra hours of work between group meetings.

Not all clubs have a Stock Selection Committee, but it

**Example: During the Beardstown Ladies'
appearance on *CBS This Morning* in November
1992, the Stock Selection Committee suggested
that we buy Cooper Tire & Rubber. Betty asked
Maxine Thomas, who was a member of the
committee, what the upside-down ratio was.
Maxine replied that it was .07, which Betty felt
was not good enough, so she suggested that we
wait and reconsider the stock at a later time.**

**Shirley Gross had different reservations
about buying the stock. She felt that we had
waited too long, that we should have bought it
several years earlier. After more discussion, we
decided against investing at that time, but to
keep an eye on Cooper Tire.**

**Last year Cooper Tire reported that its
earnings were not going to be as good as 1992.
The stock quickly fell from $33 a share to $25,
so we prepared a new Stock Selection Guide
and reconsidered. The upside-down ratio was
better than 3 to 1. Even though earnings were
down, we reasoned that people are still going to
buy good, durable tires, so we voted to buy 100
shares at 25 5/8.**

**The stock has since slid to 21 1/8, but we are
holding on. *Standard & Poor's* recently gave it a
"buy" recommendation, preferring the company
to Goodyear as an investment. We expect that
Cooper will benefit from an economic upturn
and, if it does, the shareholders will, too.**

makes participation in a club much more interesting. The
committee should select industries to investigate that will
add diversity to your portfolio. Start with *Value Line*'s list
of timely industries. Once the committee has selected an
industry, the members should consider three to five stocks

within that industry that meet the above 10 investment criteria. If the committee finds several stocks that stand above the rest, it should prepare a Stock Selection Guide (see sample, p. 114) on each one.

Making Your Selection

The Stock Selection Committee presents its recommendations to the whole club. After a thorough discussion on the merits of their argument (which is always more convincing if the committee compared the stock to others within the same industry), it is time to vote. If your committee prepares thoughtful evaluations, you will find that their recommendations are often accepted unanimously. In the absence of a consensus, the majority should rule. Sometimes a stock that is passed over one time may be purchased later on.

The Beardstown Ladies' Top 10 List

Here are our top 10 reasons for investing in a stock (with apologies to David Letterman, who is on too late for us to watch):

1. It's in the top third of its industry, as ranked by *Value Line*.
2. *Value Line* timeliness rating is 1 or 2.
3. *Value Line* safety rating is 1 or 2.
4. Total debt is no more than a third of total assets.
5. Beta falls between .90 and 1.10.
6. Five years of growth in sales and earnings, and projected growth is 12–15% in the next several years.
7. Price per share is $25 or less.
8. The price-earnings ratio is below the company's average p/e ratio for the last five years.
9. Its upside-down ratio is at least 3 to 1.
10. Competent and experienced management.

Stock Selection Guide
The most widely used aid to good investment judgment

NATIONAL ASSOCIATION OF INVESTORS CORPORATION
NAIC
INVESTMENT EDUCATION SINCE 1951

Company Colgate-Palmolive Date _____
Prepared by _____ Data taken from V-L, S+P
Where traded NYSE Major product/service _____

CAPITILIZATION	Authorized	Outstanding
Preferred		
Common		
Other Debt		Potential Dilution

1 VISUAL ANALYSIS of Sales, Earnings and Price

RECENT QUARTERLY FIGURES

	SALES	EARNINGS PER SHARE
Latest Quarter		
Year Ago Quarter		
Percentage Change		

See Chapter 14 of Investors Manual for complete instructions. Use this guide as working section of NAIC Stock Selection Guide and Report.

E/S

REVENUES

19 83 19 84 1985 19 86 19 87 1988 19 89 1990 19 91 19 92 19__ 19__ 19__ 19__

(1) Historical Sales Growth _____ %
(2) Estimated Future Sales Growth _____ %
(3) Historical Earnings Per Share Growth _____ %
(4) Estimated Future Earnings Per Share Growth _____ %

2 EVALUATING MANAGEMENT Company Colgate - Palmolive (CL)

	19 83	19 84	1985	1986	1987	1988	1989	1990	1991	1992	LAST 5 YEAR AVE.	TREND UP	DOWN
A % Pre-tax Profit on Sales (Net Before Taxes ÷ Sales)	6.9	5.5	6.1	6.0	5.9	7.9	8.9	9.0	9.2	10.4			
B % Earned on Equity (E/S÷Book Value)	14.1	12.7	16.9	18.2	22.0	20.8	37.5	32.3	26.2	21.3			

3 PRICE-EARNINGS HISTORY as an indicator of the future

		PRESENT PRICE			HIGH THIS YEAR		LOW THIS YEAR		
Year	A PRICE HIGH	B PRICE LOW	C Earnings Per Share	D Price Earnings Ratio HIGH A ÷ C	E Price Earnings Ratio LOW B ÷ C	F Dividend Per Share	G % Payout F ÷ C X 100	H % High Yield F ÷ B X 100
1	1988	24.8	19.5	1.71	14.5	11.3	0.74	43.3	3.8
2	89	32.4	22.1	1.99	16.3	11.1	0.78	39.2	3.5
3	90	37.8	26.4	2.28	16.6	11.6	0.90	39.5	3.4
4	91	49.1	33.6	2.57	19.1	13.1	1.02	39.7	3.0
5	92	60.6	45.1	2.91	20.8	15.4	1.15	39.4	2.5
6	TOTAL								
7	AVERAGE								
8	AVERAGE PRICE EARNINGS RATIO				9 CURRENT PRICE EARNINGS RATIO				

4 EVALUATING RISK and REWARD over the next 5 years

A HIGH PRICE — NEXT 5 YEARS
Avg. High P/E _____ (3B7) x Estimated High Earnings/Share _____ = Forecast High Price B-1 $ _____ (4A1)

B LOW PRICE — NEXT 5 YEARS
(a) Avg. Low P/E _____ (3B7) x Estimated Low E/Share _____ = $ _____
(b) Avg. Low Price of Last 5 Years = _____ (3B7)
(c) Recent Severe Market Low Price = _____
(d) Price Dividend Will Support Present Divd. / High Yield (H) = _____ = _____
Selected Estimated Low Price _____ B-2 $ _____ (4B1)

C ZONING
_____ (4A1) High Forecast Price Minus _____ (4B1) Low Forecast Price Equals _____ (C) Range. ⅓ of Range. = _____ (4C5)
Lower ⅓ = _____ (4B1) To _____ (Buy) (4C2)
Middle ⅓ = _____ To _____ (Maybe) (4C3)
Upper ⅓ = _____ To _____ (Sell) (4C4)
Present Market Price of _____ is in the _____ (4C5) Range

D UP-SIDE DOWN-SIDE RATIO (Potential Gain vs. Risk of Loss)
High Price _____ (4A1) Minus Present Price _____ = _____ = _____ To 1
Present Price _____ Minus Low Price _____ (4B1) _____ (4D)

5 5-YEAR POTENTIAL

A Present Full Year's Dividend $ _____ = _____ x 100 = _____ Present Yield or % Returned on Purchase Price
Present Price of Stock $ _____

B AVERAGE YIELD OVER NEXT 5 YEARS
Avg. Earn. Per Share Next 5 Years _____ x Avg. % Payout _____ = _____ = _____ %
Present Price $ _____

© 1991. National Association of Investors Corporation; 1515 E. Eleven Mile Road, Royal Oak, MI 48067

The Companies We Keep

Here is a list of the stocks we own (as of 5/31/94), and a very brief explanation of why we bought each one. Of course, all of them met our basic investment criteria (see Chapter 13) as well.

A. G. Edwards, a brokerage firm. We believed that more and more people would be investing in the stock market. Because this firm caters to individual investors, we thought it would benefit from the trend.

Casey's General Stores, convenience store chain. Opened several stores in our area that seemed to be well run and popular.

Century Telephone, small telephone company. Good growth prospects.

Cifra S.A. de C.V. Adr., the "Wal-Mart of Mexico." We expected the Mexican economy to improve.

Cooper Tire & Rubber, tire manufacturer. People are holding on to cars longer and need replacement tires.

Glaxo Holdings, a pharmaceutical company. We wanted to get into the drug industry, and at $17 a share, it was affordable. We also were impressed by several of its products.

Hershey Foods, candy manufacturer. We all love chocolate. This company appeared to be well managed and poised for double-digit growth.

Home Depot, building materials supply store. Great growth record and well managed. With recent earthquakes and flooding, we expected continued growth.

Our Best and Worst Stock Picks

The Top Performers

W. A. KRUGER: One of our first real successes was investing in W. A. Kruger, a small company that publishes magazines. The club bought 100 shares in July 1984. At the time we paid $8 a share, plus a $30 commission.

Sixteen months later, the stock price had risen to 15 3/8. We got new information from *Value Line* and the stock was not projected to go past 16. Since we wanted to see 100% appreciation, we put in a sell order at 16, directing our broker to sell our shares if the price reached $16 per share. During the month it hit 16 and we sold our shares for $1,600 minus a $40.36 commission. Our total return was 88% over 16 months, or an annual return of 66%. Counting dividends, our annual return was 70.2%. We were real proud of ourselves because we did what we set out to do.

RPM: Shirley was on the Stock Selection Committee that recommended this winner after reading about it in *Value Line*. An Ohio-based manufacturer of protective coatings and paints, RPM has had 46 years of consecutive record sales and 19 years of consecutive cash dividend increases. It is currently our largest holding.

We started out with 35 shares in December 1984 and added another 65 shares the following February. With several splits (additional shares issued for each outstanding share) and additional purchases, we have accumulated 300 shares. Our total return on these shares through February 1994 is 271%.

The company is known for growing through acquisitions of complementary companies, such as RustOleum B.V. of the Netherlands, and leaving competent managers in place. "I liked it from the beginning," says Ruth Huston, who follows the stock for the club. "It's a steady stock, a stock to hold. When they buy a new business, they keep the old managers, which saves lots of work for the central office."

CPI: We invested $750 in 45 shares of CPI, which operates portrait studios for Sears, in April 1985. We received another 45 shares through a stock split in March 1987. Since the price was cut in half, we bought another 10 shares for $242 to give us an even lot.

In June 1990 we prepared a new stock selection guide, determined that the price may have hit a peak at $31.50, and decided to sell. (We followed it for some time after that and we were right.) Our capital gain when we sold was $2,075.47, giving us a total return of 209% in five years.

WOLVERINE WORLDWIDE: We bought 50 shares of this Michigan-based maker of workboots and casual shoes in April 1992 because we felt that women were wearing more practical shoes to work and Wolverine was well positioned to take advantage of that change in the market. Farmers have been wearing Wolverine boots for years, so we were familiar with the high quality of its products. When the price fell seven months later, we took the opportunity to add another 150 shares. So far our return has been 184%.

The Ladies' Lemons

FUR VAULT: This was, without a doubt, our biggest loss during our 10-year history. We bought 100 shares for $1,178.64, including commission, in April 1987. The next winter was warm and protests against people who wore fur began to get lots of media attention. The stock fell nearly 50% and showed no prospects of recovery, but we held on, reluctant to hurt the feelings of the partner who had recommended it.

We finally sold our shares in October 1989 at a loss of $853.66. That translates into a total loss of 72.4%, or a 29% loss on an annual basis. The thought of it still gives us shivers.

WENDY'S: After following this company for several months, we bought 39 shares for $23.04 per share in December 1983, and another 48 shares the following May. At the time we noted that its earnings per share had enjoyed an upward rise and price projections by *Value Line* were for 8% to 15% growth over the next several years.

There were some ways that it didn't quite meet our standards, however. Its price-earnings ratio was 22, slightly higher than the five-year average of 18.8. Its upside-down ratio was only 1.6 to 1. Timeliness was 2, but safety was 3.

After we invested, it had a couple of splits and was riding up, doing very nicely. Then the restaurants started offering breakfasts and got into some trouble. Part of their problem, we thought, was that they were cooking to order. If you ordered hot cakes, for instance, you waited; if they were very busy, you waited a long time.

Aunt Margaret, who was following Wendy's for the club, came back from Florida in 1984 and told us that she noticed its restaurants were not as busy as they had been before and maybe this was a warning. But it had done so well for us we discarded that thought and held on to it. We let it go down to 5 5/8 per share before we sold our stock and ate a loss of $699.21—a drop of 55.8%, or 11% on an annual basis.

After we sold our Wendy's stock, the price started to climb again. Now it's back up to 17 1/2.

Our Portfolio - 9/94

No. of shares	Security	Price/share*	Total cost	Price per share 9/12/94
200	Casey's General Stores	$11.80	$2360.80	$11.00
50	Century Telephone	26.70	1335.17	29.25
1000	Cifra	3.38	3375.70	3.02
100	Cooper Tire & Rubber	25.62	2562.44	26.00
100	Cracker Barrel	26.14	2614.02	24.13
125	A.G. Edwards	9.76	1220.16	19.25
100	Glaxo Holdings	8.92	892.23	19.00
100	Hershey Foods	32.72	3272.32	44.63
100	Home Depot	41.88	4187.99	44.00
100	Merck & Co.	42.06	4206.42	33.63
200	McDonald's	14.69	2937.83	27.38
100	PepsiCo	32.88	3287.77	33.13
100	Quaker Oats	72.74	7274.19	80.25
150	Rollins	11.11	1666.63	25.25
300	RPM	6.99	2096.74	18.00
100	Rubbermaid	32.20	3220.03	27.25
200	Shaw Industries	18.06	3611.84	15.50
100	St. Jude Medical	34.00	3399.79	35.75

Our Portfolio - 9/94

No. of shares	Security	Price/share*	Total cost	Price per share 9/12/94
150	VeriFone	21.37	3204.97	21.00
200	Wal-Mart	15.42	3084.64	25.38
100	WMX Technologies	33.59	3359.14	28.38
300	Wolverine Worldwide	8.32	2495.33	26.63

*Includes cost of commission.

Lawter Intl., maker of printing ink. Met our investment criteria.

McDonalds, fast-food king. Great growth prospects.

Merck & Co., leading drug company. We wanted to invest in the pharmaceutical industry and this stock hit a price we could afford.

PepsiCo, diversified food manufacturer and restaurant operator. We like all their products and restaurants, including Pepsi, Kentucky Fried Chicken, Taco Bell, and Frito Lay snack foods.

Quaker Oats, food company based in Illinois. We were familiar with its products and liked what we were reading in the press about the company.

Rollins, lawn care and pest-control company. Many of our members were familiar with the company; it had no debt and projected double-digit growth.

RPM, an Ohio-based manufacturer of protective coatings and paints. The company has an extremely long record of increasing sales and dividends.

Rubbermaid, manufacturer of plastic and rubber products. A double-digit growth record; products that we know and use.

St. Jude Medical, leading manufacturer of heart valves. It had no debt.

Shaw Industries, leading carpet manufacturer. With rebuilding after floods and earthquakes, we expected increased sales.

VeriFone, manufacturer of automatic transaction systems. One of the few stocks our broker recommended.

Wal-Mart, leading discount store. Opened a store in Beardstown where the parking lot was always full.

WMX Technologies, waste management company. A leading company in an area of growing concern.

Wolverine Worldwide, shoe manufacturer. We were familiar with its high-quality workboots. With women wearing more sensible shoes to work, we expected sales of its women's line to grow.

> **"When we purchase a stock, we buy it at a price that we think is favorable and we expect 100% appreciation in the next three to five years."**
>
> **—BETTY SINNOCK**

14. How to Know If the Price Is Right: Simple Stock Evaluation Methods

You already know the importance of *time* to an investor who studies the fundamentals: First you find a company with a strong balance sheet, experienced management, and promising growth prospects; then you must be patient and hold on for the long term, giving the company and its stock price ample time to grow.

But *timing* does count for something, too. Even if you have identified a stock that has good growth prospects in an industry with explosive expansion, you need to check on your timing. If you have discovered the stock too late, you may pay a price that has already been bid up by other investors.

This is particularly true of booming companies that have gotten lots of publicity. Often their stock prices are quickly bid up by investors anxious to profit from expected growth. Take the example of Boston Chicken, a popular chain of roasted chicken fast-food outlets that sold its first stock to the public (called an *initial public offering*) in the fall of 1993.

Boston Chicken's stock opened at $20 and flew up to more than $48 in the first few hours. If you added together the value of the common stock outstanding at that price, it was worth far more than the underlying company; a sure sign that the price would fall once all the excitement wore off. That's exactly what happened, and the stock is now trading at $35.75. Those investors who anticipated the growth of the company but who had the poor timing to buy it at $48 may have to hold on for many years before they see any growth in their investment.

Because a club's objective is to double its holdings every five years, members should restrict their purchases to stocks whose price is likely to rise a hefty 100% over that period, taking care to avoid those that have already done so and probably won't go much further. Naturally there is no way to predict future price appreciation with certainty, but you can make an educated guess.

Estimated Price Appreciation

The first step is to consult the latest *Value Line Investment Survey* write-up on the stock you are studying. This tracks each stock's high and low price for the past decade right at the top of the page. The high and the low prices hit during the last five years can give you a rough approximation of what the stock's range might be in the next 12 months.

If the current price is near the five-year high, you should think twice about investing at this time. If you firmly believe in its growth prospects, however, the club might agree to watch the stock and buy it at a later point if the price falls back closer to the five-year average.

You can also consult *Value Line's* projections for price appreciation, both a high and low, for the next three to five years. Is the price projected to rise 100% or close to that by the end of five years? If the answer is yes, and the projected low also represents healthy growth, say 60% or more, this stock may be a good bet.

> **Example: Company X's common shares are currently trading at $10 a share. *Value Line* projects that in five years the stock will be trading for between $16 and $20 a share. The projected low ($16) is 60% higher than the current price. This stock may be a good investment.**

Earnings per Share

Earnings per share is another measure worth considering. Are earnings per share growing at the same rate as sales? These figures are easily found in a small box marked "Annual Rates" on the left side of the *Value Line* sheet. There you will find the "annual rate of change per share" for the past 10 years, for the past five years, and estimated for the next five years for both sales and earnings.

Simply compare these percentages for sales and earnings. If they are pretty close, this is an excellent sign because it indicates that the company is growing its profits at the same rate it grows its sales.

If, instead, sales are growing much faster than earnings, then the growth is not benefiting shareholders as much as we like to see.

> **Example: In *Value Line*'s write-up on Rubbermaid (10/22/93), the company's annual rate of change per share for the past 10 years was 19% for earnings, 13.5% for sales. For the past five years, it was 16% for earnings, 13% for sales. For the next three to five years, it was estimated to see 15.5% growth in earnings, 11.5% for sales. Earnings have been growing even faster than sales for the last 10 years and that trend is expected to continue. We consider this a big plus, even though we know this cannot continue forever since earnings come from sales.**

If you can purchase a share for the sum of the estimated earnings per share for the next five years (*Value Line* projects these, too), that is another positive indicator. When comparing stocks in the same industry, we like to buy the company where the sum of the five-year projected earnings is closer percentage wise to the current price.

> **Example: Company Y is selling for $5 a share. *Value Line* projects that in the next five years, its earnings per share will be $1, $2, $0.50, $0.50 and $0.25, or a total of $4.25.**

Dividends

A promising growth company should pay out no more than half of its earnings in dividends; the rest should be plowed back into the company to fuel further growth. If a company has a track record of paying out 4–6% of its current stock price in dividends, and still has at least half of its earnings left over to invest in its business, you may indeed have spotted a winner.

> **Example: Working this out doesn't take too
> much fancy figuring. Take a look at *Value Line*'s
> write-up on Rubbermaid again. In the very
> bottom left-hand corner are two boxes listing
> "EARNINGS PER SHARE" and "QUARTERLY
> DIVIDENDS PAID" for the last five calendar
> years. If you compare them, you will see that
> Rubbermaid earned $0.90 per share in 1990, yet
> paid $0.27 that year in dividends, less than one-
> third of its earnings. That trend continues
> through 1992, the latest year comparative
> figures are available on this sheet. This is a
> promising sign.**
>
> **On the other hand, if you look at the stock's
> average annual dividend yield, it has remained
> below 4% for the last 15 years and is not
> expected to go above 1.5% in the upcoming
> couple of years. But because we are more
> concerned about growth than dividends, we
> would probably weigh the earnings per share
> results more heavily than the dividend yield.**

Book Value

Comparing a stock's book value to its current price may also
be a clue to the appropriateness of the price. To calculate
book value, subtract current liabilities from current assets.
Then divide by the number of common shares to get the
book value per share. (These numbers can be found in *Value
Line*; but for a real short cut, simply look at their chart,
which has already done the work for you, calculating "book
value per share" for the past 15 years and projected for the
next three to five.) If the book value per share is much lower
than the price per share, you may be looking at a stock that
is overpriced.

(Book value per share should never be the only number

you base your decision on, however, because a company may overstate or underestimate the value of some of its assets. Unless you are extremely familiar with a company, you may be unable to detect inaccuracies.)

Price-Earnings Ratio

Close examination of a company's price-earnings ratio is more useful. First, track a stock's price-earnings ratio for the past five years. (We usually fill this information in on NAIC's Stock Selection Guide, which is an excellent tool to use when studying stocks to buy.)

Next, determine the stock's average p/e's (found in *Value Line*) for each of the past five years, add them up and divide by five to get the average p/e. Avoid the stock if its current p/e is higher than its average p/e.

Example: Take Company Z. The stock's average p/e ratios for the last five years were 11.2; 9.8; 10.8; 7.9; and 10. Today's p/e ratio is 15. It may not be an ideal time to invest in this company.

Peter Lynch, the revered mutual fund manager, suggests comparing a stock's p/e ratio with its growth rate. If they are about equal, he considers the stock fairly priced. If it is less than the growth rate, "you may have found yourself a bargain," he writes in his book *One Up on Wall Street*. "In general, a p/e ratio that's half the growth rate is very positive, and one that's twice the growth rate is very negative."

None of these measures can tell you precisely what the right price is. But buying a stock *before* you study its prospects for price appreciation would most certainly be poor timing.

15. When to Sell: Doing Your Homework and Getting It Right

Deciding when to sell is one of the most difficult judgments investors have to make. It can feel like walking a tightrope, trying to strike a balance between selling too soon and holding on too long.

Most amateur investors, however, tend to tip toward selling stocks prematurely. If a stock dips below the price you paid for it or if the market heads south, and you feel the temptation to sell immediately: resist. Remember, you made your purchases only after closely examining each stock. Reversing that decision should not be done without first making another careful study of its prospects. You may discover that a drop in price is a good opportunity to buy more shares of a company that has strong fundamentals and plenty of growth prospects.

On the other hand, investment clubs are sometimes guilty of holding on to nonperforming stocks for sentimental reasons, because of an attachment to the company or to avoid hurting the feelings of the club member who recommended it. Each investment decision was made by the entire group; individual members should receive neither credit nor blame. We learned this firsthand! Take a look at our disaster with Fur Vault for proof (p. 117).

When thinking of selling a stock, there are two primary indicators to consider:

1. It is performing below your expectations; or
2. it has met or exceeded your expectations ahead of schedule, and future growth prospects have diminished.

If a Stock Is Performing Below Expectations

If a stock's price remains flat or continues to drop for several months, it is time to reevaluate your investment. Consult *Value Line* and *Standard & Poor's* to determine whether the high ratings and growth projections that led you to purchase the stock have been adjusted downward.

If the company's financial strength, management, and other fundamentals continue to be strong and there is continued prospect for growth, try to determine what is exerting downward pressure on the price. Perhaps it is being held down by bad news that you believe will have only a temporary effect. If so, you can continue to hold the stock with confidence. Of course, if the price continues to slide for several more months, you should again reconsider.

If your research shows that the company's fundamentals are weak, with little or no prospect for improvement, it is probably wise to sell, even if it means incurring a loss. If you do not divest, you risk losing even more. If instead you redirect your money to a more promising investment, you can greatly increase your chance for further profitability.

> **Example: We sold Harland, incurring a loss of $195.36, because we didn't feel it was performing up to our expectations, and bought 100 shares of McDonald's, which is still growing strong.**

If a Stock Has Met or Exceeded Your Expectations

When you buy a stock, you should have a price in mind that you expect it to reach within five years (typically double the purchase price). When it hits that price, even if it's ahead of schedule, reevaluate the stock. If the company's fundamentals are still strong, and there is lots of growth potential, hold on to it. If the fundamentals are weak, it's time to bail out.

> **Example: We bought W. A. Kruger, a publishing company, at $8 a share. Sixteen months later, the stock was up to 15 3/8, but *Value Line* predicted no further price appreciation. We sold at 16.**

Many other events may spur you to consider selling as an option. The following list is adapted from NAIC's *Investors' Manual*.

Adverse management changes: Any changes in upper management of a company may signal a change in its fortunes. Watch the popular press for articles that chronicle the reasons for change and how the new managers are perceived by the investment community. You might ask if your broker has any information about the new personnel or if there are any analysts' reports that can be sent to you.

Competition is adversely affecting the company's prosperity: If competitors are doing a better job of merchandising their products, or a key product has become obsolete because a competitor has developed a more attractive substitute, you should reevaluate your position in a stock. Growth may have come to a complete halt.

A company depends on a single product and "that rose has lost its bloom": A company that has not diversified must be carefully tracked.

Example: We bought 100 shares of Archer Daniels Midland, (ADM), which we consider a very good company, in April 1990. But when ADM put so much stake in ethanol and it was questionable whether they would be able to profit from it, we reconsidered our position. Earnings predictability and other measures were not as favorable as they had been, and we decided that this was the time to sell. We sold it for a small profit of $122. The stock price later dropped and it hasn't yet been back up to what we sold it for.

Declining profit margins or deteriorating financial structure: If profit margins shrink during one quarter, it is possible that earnings will remain depressed for many more months. A sudden increase in debt is also a warning signal. If the company has no plans that are plausible for reversing these conditions, selling might be worth considering. Occasionally management-employee relations become so sour that the profitability of a company becomes endangered.

Example: Central Illinois Power Service Company (CIPSCO) locked out its employees in summer 1993. The company also had to pay several million dollars back to its customers because of excessive income. One of our members suggested it didn't have the cash reserves that it had in the past, and very possibly would not be able to sustain its pre-tax profits. We had a good profit, so we decided this was the time to get out. We sold at $32.50 a share and we are glad we did. A year later, it's selling for $26.50.

The NAIC also has a useful list of Selling Don'ts:

1. Don't sell just because the price hasn't moved. As long as the fundamentals are strong, have patience.

2. Don't sell because of a paper loss. (A "paper loss" or "paper profit" is a loss or profit that you would make if you sold your stock at a particular price. These gains or losses are nothing more than calculations made on a piece of paper; they do not become "real" until your stock is actually sold. *Example: If you bought 10 shares of a stock at $10 a share and the stock fell to $5, you would have a paper loss of $50. If you held on to the stock another month and the price rose to $6 before you sold it, your actual loss would be $40.*) Again, focus on the fundamentals, not a declining market, which may pull the prices of strong stocks down in the short run.

3. Don't sell because of a paper profit. If you sell automatically when a stock hits a predetermined price, you risk missing out on even more profit. If the fundamentals and growth prospects remain strong, don't part with that stock!

4. Don't sell on temporary bad news. If the long-term view looks bright, hold on for the ride.

5. Don't sell just to take action. Holding is as meaningful an action as buying or selling.

6. Don't sell a stock that has fallen so far that your remaining downside risk is small compared to the upside potential. You might have nowhere to go but up.

16. Our Club's Method of Dollar Cost Averaging: A Long-term Investment Tool

Buying stocks when the market picks up, and avoiding the market when it turns downward, is like buying underwear at Marshall Field's when you can get the same brand at Wal-Mart. There's a good chance that you'll be paying more than you need to.

"Dollar cost averaging," popular with conservative, long-term investors, is a stock-purchasing technique to make sure you pay Wal-Mart prices. Dollar cost averaging requires making regular purchases of a particular stock or set of stocks with a set sum regardless of the market's level. When stock prices dip, you will receive more shares for your money; when stock prices rise, you will receive fewer shares. Over an extended period of time during which stocks have moved both up and down, you will find that your average price per share is lower than the average price for that period. The mathematical reason: Simply because you bought more shares when prices were low and fewer shares when prices were high.

Dollar cost averaging is particularly appropriate for a club or individual just beginning to build a portfolio. In addition to establishing a regular pattern of investing, it adds to the power of your initial investment dollars. New clubs might consider picking several stocks to start with and investing in them regularly during the first year. (Don't forget to figure in commission costs. One strategy is to save up enough dues to purchase 100 shares every few months.)

For our club, applying a less strict method of dollar cost averaging works better. We do not invest a set amount in a specific stock during a set interval. Instead, we are committed to investing during the market's ups and downs, so long as we have found a stock with good value. Over our 10 years together, we have lowered our average costs per share simply by adding to our investments in market dips. If you remain committed to investing when the market takes its periodic nose dives, you can decrease your average costs per share, too.

> **"It's so important not to kill the goose that's laying the golden egg after the first egg. We don't take money out. If you take it out, you really defeat yourself."**
>
> **—BUFFY TILLITT-PRATT**

17. The Power of Reinvesting

Investors looking for income view dividends—the portion of profits that companies divide up among their stockholders—as a critical contribution to their bank account. But growth-oriented investors like us look at them much differently.

For one thing, we do not want management to part with more than half of their "retained earnings," profits left after taxes. Our thinking is this: Shareholders will probably benefit much more in the long run if profits are poured back into the business (in an efficient manner, of course) to help it prosper and expand.

When we do receive dividend checks, which over the

course of a year can amount to roughly 5% of the stock price for strong growth companies, we view them as seed money, funds that will lead to a bigger yield of profit at some future harvest. We quickly plow them back into our portfolio.

Automatically reinvesting your dividends is an excellent method of ensuring continued, steady investment growth over time. Using these funds to add to your investment naturally is one of the best and easiest ways to build up your portfolio. And you will be compounding your income because you will garner income from your initial investment and from the income itself (see the Dividend Reinvestment chart, page 137).

Given time, dividends can add up to significant totals. Remember the case of the Mutual Investment Club of Detroit. Over 52 years, members invested a total of $291,045 in individual contributions. Dividends alone gave them another $651,751 to invest. The result was a portfolio that, after withdrawals of $1,310,411, was valued at $2,109,917.

Many people whose portfolios are diminutive in comparison reinvest regularly. Frequently they invest their dividends in the same stock that generated them. This is a sensible strategy, particularly if you invest in the many companies that have set up automatic reinvestment plans that add to your holdings without charging commissions.

Our method of reinvesting is more suitable for a club that holds a wide portfolio of stocks. We place our dividends in a cash account with our broker, so that they will automatically be applied to our next stock purchase. That way they are usually reinvested shortly after they are received, but we maintain the freedom to direct where they will be invested.

We prefer this method to automatically reinvesting in the same stock because oftentimes a stock that was in a "buy" range when we bought it, while still good to hold, does not offer as much value to the new purchaser at a later time.

Dividend Reinvestment Chart

Month	Amount paid in	Dividend added	Total invested	Shares purchased	Total shares owned
1	$ 20	—	$ 20.00	1.333	1.333
2	20	$ 0.27	20.27	1.267	2.600
3	20	—	20.00	1.176	3.776
4	20	—	20.00	1.250	5.026
5	20	1.00	21.00	1.400	6.426
6	20	—	20.00	1.428	7.854
7	20	—	20.00	1.538	9.392
8	20	1.88	21.88	1.563	10.955
9	20	—	20.00	1.333	12.288
10	20	—	20.00	1.428	13.716
11	20	2.74	22.74	1.749	15.465
12	20	—	20.00	1.667	17.132
13	20	—	20.00	1.818	18.950
14	20	3.79	23.79	1.983	20.933
15	20	—	20.00	1.538	22.471
16	20	—	20.00	1.667	24.138
17	20	4.83	24.83	1.910	26.048
18	20	—	20.00	1.428	27.476
19	20	—	20.00	1.333	28.809
20	20	5.76	25.76	1.610	30.419
21	20	—	20.00	1.176	31.595
22	20	—	20.00	1.111	32.706
Totals	$440	$20.27	$460.27	32.706	@$18 = $588.71

SOURCE: Reprinted with permission from the National Association of Investors Corporation.

In addition, because the main purpose of our club is education, and we learn most by the exercise of studying and choosing new stocks, we would rather not restrict our purchases to those that came before. (Of course, we always compare new investments with those we already have. It is not unusual for us to buy additional shares at a later time if they still offer exceptional value.)

Whatever you decide to do with your dividends as an individual or in conjunction with your club, just make sure you reinvest them! When harvest time comes you will be glad that you did.

Reinvesting Dividends

Compounding income results from *reinvesting earnings*. Income is then received on both savings and earnings on those savings. The additional amount earned is small at first, but grows to sizable sums as investing continues. In the case illustrated on page 137, by reinvesting earnings over 22 months, the investor ended up with 32.706 shares, roughly 1½ more shares than she would have owned had she not reinvested.

Part Three

THE BEARDSTOWN LADIES

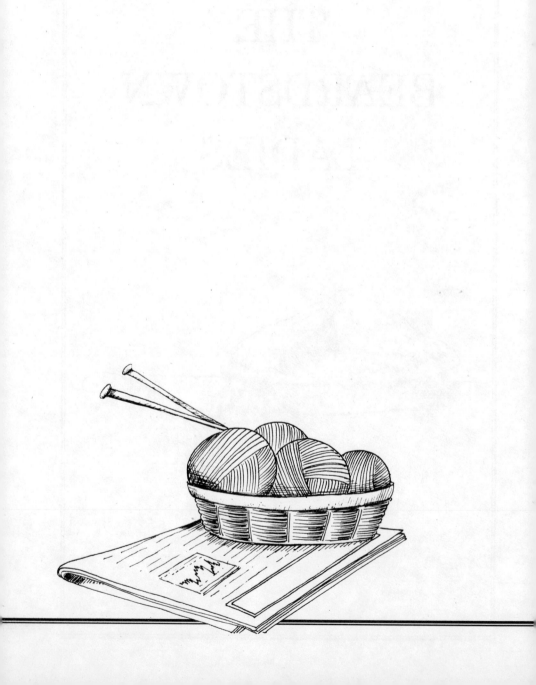

> "*Our banner year was 1991, when the club's return on its stocks traded on the New York Stock Exchange was 59.5%, more than 10 times the S&P 500's performance during the same period. The entire portfolio's return was 53%.*
>
> *Here are highlights of our meetings and monthly copies of our portfolio. You will see that we stuck to our conservative approach—buying and holding only the best-performing stocks we could find, and evaluating our portfolio on a monthly basis.*"
>
> **—SYLVIA GAUSHELL**

18. How We Made 59.5%, Month-by-Month

The Companies We Kept in 1991

Here are brief descriptions of the companies that we owned during 1991, and the reasons why we bought them. We parted ways with several of them before the end of the year; others we still hold.

A. G. Edwards, a brokerage firm. We believed that more and more people would be investing in the stock market. Because this firm caters to individual investors, we thought it would benefit from the trend.

Archer Daniels Midland, an Illinois-based miller of corn, soybeans, and flour. It had good growth prospects at home and abroad.

Baxter, an Illinois-based health care company. It was a major supplier of intravenous equipment, which we considered a growth area.

Calgon Carbon, a major distributor of water purifiers. We thought its growth prospects were good.

CIPSCO, our local gas and electric utility. We knew the company well and it was a growth stock while we held it.

Gannett, a media company. We wanted to get into the newspaper industry and were impressed by *USA Today*, its national publication.

Glaxo Holdings, the pharmaceutical company. We wanted to get into the drug industry, and at $17 a share it was affordable. We were also impressed by its product Zantec.

Harland, a leading producer of checks. It met all our investment criteria and looked very promising.

Hershey Foods, candy manufacturer. We all love chocolate. It appeared to be well managed and poised for double-digit growth.

Lawter Intl., maker of printing ink. Met our investment criteria.

McDonalds, fast-food king. Great growth prospects.

PepsiCo, diversified food manufacturer and restaurant operator. We like all their products and restaurants, including Pepsi, Kentucky Fried Chicken, Taco Bell, and Frito Lay snack foods.

Rollins, lawn care and pest-control company. Many of our members were familiar with the company; it had no debt and projected double-digit growth.

RPM, the Ohio-based manufacturer of protective coatings and paints. The company has an extremely long record of increasing sales and dividends.

St. Jude Medical, leading manufacturer of heart valves. It had no debt.

Smithfield Foods, pork producer. We wanted to get into this industry because one of our members is so familiar with it. This company seemed promising because it is involved in both raising hogs and processing them for market.

VeriFone, manufacturer of automatic transaction systems. One of the few stocks our broker recommended.

Wal-Mart, leading discount store. Opened a store in Beardstown and its parking lot was always full.

Zero, a manufacturer of plastic products and refrigeration and heating equipment. Was poised for future growth.

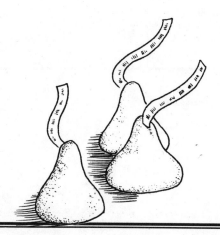

Our Portfolio, 12/31/90

Stock	Number of shares	Purchase price per share*	Current price	*ValueLine's* timeliness / safety
A. G. Edwards	110	22⅞	20⅜	3/3
Archer Daniels Midland	105	23¾	22¾	3/2
Baxter	100	21⅝	27⅞	2/3
Calgon Carbon	25	42⅝	43¼	2/3
CIPSCO	100	23¼	21¾	3/1
Gannett	100	37⅜	36⅛	3/1
Glaxo Holdings	100	17⅞	32¾	1/2
Harland	100	21⅜	19⅛	3/2
Hershey Foods	100	32¾	37½	2/2
Lawter Intl.	133	9⅞	11¼	2/3
Rollins	100	16⅝	21¼	2/3
RPM	250	10⅜	17½	3/3
St. Jude Medical	50	35⅝	34½	2/3
Wal-Mart	100	30⅞	30¼	1/2
Zero	125	15¾	11¼	4/3

*Purchase price includes commission.

January 1991

We began the year with a meeting at Hardee's restaurant in Beardstown and a portfolio balance of $37,430.06. Lillian Ellis reported that economists' forecasts for 1991 were real conservative, but that didn't dampen our enthusiasm for the market a bit!

Our Portfolio, 1/31/91

Stock	Number of shares	Purchase price per share*	Current price	*Value Line's* timeliness / safety
A. G. Edwards	110	23	24½	3/3
Archer Daniels Midland	105	23¾	20⅜	3/2
Baxter	100	21⅝	29½	2/3
Calgon Carbon	25	42⅝	41¾	2/3
CIPSCO	100	23¼	22	3/1
Gannett	100	37⅜	40⅞	3/1
Glaxo Holdings	100	17⅞	35⅝	1/2
Harland	100	21⅜	19¾	3/2
Hershey Foods	100	32¾	39¾	2/2
Lawter Intl.	133	9⅞	12	2/3
Rollins	100	16⅝	20¾	2/3
RPM	250	10⅜	17⅞	2/3
St. Jude Medical	50	35⅝	39¼	1/3
Wal-Mart	100	30⅞	33	1/2
Zero	125	15¾	11⅞	4/3

February 1991

We met at Shirley Gross's home, which is quite a bit cozier than Hardee's. Our balance had grown to $41,131.12, with 11 stocks out of 15 making gains during the past month.

After a coffee break, the Stock Selection Committee reported on McDonald's, PepsiCo, AT&T, ConAgra, and Westinghouse. Noting that Harland didn't seem to be going anywhere and had little growth potential, and the McDonald's Corp. stock price was down in the buy range and had more growth prospects, Buffy Tillitt-Pratt made a motion to sell 100 shares of Harland and to buy 100 shares of McDonald's. Buffy added that the McDonald's *Value Line* ratings were excellent: 2 for timeliness; 1 for safety: A$^+$ for financial strength. Seconded by Shirley Gross, the motion carried.

Several members pre-paid their dues for next month to make sure there was enough money to buy the McDonald's stock.

Our Portfolio, 2/28/91

Stock	Number of shares	Purchase price per share	Current price	*Value Line*'s timeliness/ safety
A. G. Edwards	110	22⅞	29½	1/2
Archer Daniels Midland	105	23¾	22¼	3/2
Baxter	100	21⅝	31¼	2/3
Calgon Carbon	25	42⅝	50½	2/3
CIPSCO	100	23¼	22¾	3/1
Gannett	100	37⅜	38⅝	3/1
Glaxo Holdings	100	17⅞	37⅞	1/2
Hershey Foods	100	32¾	39⅞	2/2
Lawter Intl.	133	9⅞	13½	2/3
McDonald's	100	29⅜	31⅝	2/1
Rollins	100	16⅝	22⅝	2/3
RPM	250	10⅜	20½	2/3
St. Jude Medical	50	35⅝	44¾	2/3
Wal-Mart	100	30⅞	35⅜	1/2
Zero	125	15¾	11⅞	4/3

March 1991

Back at Hardee's again. Our portfolio balance is up 10% over last month to $45,282.79. Because of our McDonald's purchase, our cash on hand is only $69.40.

Noting that the stock was not performing as expected and the company's growth had stalled, we sold our Harland stock on 2/8/91 for a total of $1,937.22 and a loss of $195.36. McDonald's was bought for $29.378 a share.

We made plans to attend a regional investment seminar next month. Being rather conservative with our money, we tried to get six or more members to sign up early so the cost of the lunch and program would be reduced from $12 to $10.50 each.

Stock Selection Committee member Ann Brewer reported on Sara Lee. She thought it was an excellent company, and noted its diversity. But between the time she studied it and the meeting, the price had risen, so she felt it was now too high to buy. Doris Edwards discussed National Service Industries, a highly diversified company that makes lighting equipment and water treatment chemicals and rents textiles. She noted that its timeliness rating was a 3 and that *Value Line* projected that this year might be the first in 15 that the company would not increase its earnings.

Since we do not have enough money to purchase any stock, we made no investment decisions. We will continue to follow stocks that were presented and continue to look for others.

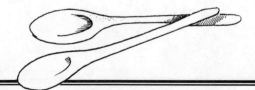

Our Portfolio, 3/31/91

Stock	Number of shares	Purchase price per share	Current price	*Value Line's* timeliness / safety
A. G. Edwards	110	22⅞	32⅜	3/3
Archer Daniels Midland	105	23¾	22	3/2
Baxter	100	21⅝	33¼	2/3
Calgon Carbon	25	42⅝	51¼	2/3
CIPSCO	100	23¼	23¼	4/1
Gannett	100	37⅜	40½	3/1
Glaxo Holdings	100	17⅞	39⅝	1/2
Hershey Foods	100	32¾	40⅞	2/2
Lawter Intl.	133	9⅞	14¼	2/3
McDonald's	100	29⅜	34¾	2/1
Rollins	100	16⅝	24	2/3
RPM	250	10⅜	20⅞	2/3
St. Jude Medical	50	35⅝	48¾	1/3
Wal-Mart	100	30⅞	38¾	1/2
Zero	125	15¾	13	4/3

April 1991

Our portfolio balance is up to $47,808.04, an increase of 5.5%.

A collection was taken to buy a clock for our broker, Homer Rieken, to show our appreciation for his help. It will be presented to him at the next Beardstown Business and Professional Women's Club meeting, where he will be guest speaker.

Maxine Thomas, junior partner, announced that a number of our club's stocks had been listed in *Better Investing*'s list of Top 100 stocks.

Our cash balance is not much more than $480, so we skipped the report from the Stock Selection Committee.

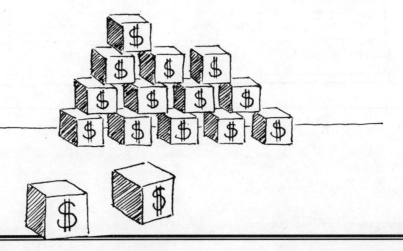

Our Portfolio, 4/30/91

Stock	Number of shares	Purchase price per share	Current price	*Value Line's* timeliness / safety
A. G. Edwards	110	22⅞	33	2/3
Archer Daniels Midland	105	23¾	22⅞	3/2
Baxter	100	21⅝	34⅜	2/3
Calgon Carbon	25	42⅝	52¼	2/3
CIPSCO	100	23¼	24½	3/1
Gannett	100	37⅜	42½	4/1
Glaxo Holdings	100	17⅞	38⅛	2/2
Hershey Foods	100	32¾	40⅛	2/2
Lawter Intl.	133	9⅞	13⅝	2/3
McDonald's	100	29⅜	33½	2/1
Rollins	100	16⅝	24⅛	2/3
RPM	250	10⅜	20¾	2/3
St. Jude Medical	50	35⅝	41½	1/3
Wal-Mart	100	30⅞	40½	1/2
Zero	125	15¾	14⅛	4/3

May 1991

Hardee's is getting to be a habit. The value of the portfolio has dipped a bit to $47,357.81, with eight stocks out of 15 losing ground.

Marilyn Ritter submitted her resignation from the club, which prompted a discussion of whether to sell a stock at a profit or sell a stock not doing so well to buy out her share. Since RPM was our largest holding, Carnell Korsmeyer made a motion to sell 50 shares of RPM and 125 shares of Zero Corp., whose *Value Line* timeliness rating has dropped to 4. Seconded by Doris Edwards, the motion carried. This will be enough to cover Marilyn's share with our cash account. Marilyn's capital gain in her partner's account was 61%.

Stock Selection Committee member Ann Brewer reported on Sara Lee but didn't recommend it because we didn't have enough money to buy any stock. Doris Edwards reported on Services Industries but didn't recommend it for the same reason. Betty said she had talked to Homer Rieken, who thought we might be interested in Veritone [sic]. No decisions were made, so the Stock Selection Committee will serve for another month.

Our Portfolio, 5/31/91				
Stock	**Number of shares**	**Purchase price per share**	**Current price**	***Value Line's* timeliness/safety**
A.G. Edwards	110	22⅞	35½	2/3
Archer Daniels Midland	105	23¾	22½	3/2
Baxter	100	21⅝	34½	2/3
Calgon Carbon	25	42⅝	57¼	2/3
CIPSCO	100	23¼	23½	3/1
Gannett	100	37⅜	44⅜	4/1
Glaxo Holdings	100	17⅞	40¾	2/2
Hershey Foods	100	32⅞	43⅞	2/2
Lawter Intl.	133	9⅞	13	2/3
McDonald's	100	29⅜	35	2/1
Rollins	100	16⅝	23⅞	2/3
RPM	200	10⅝	22¼	2/3
St. Jude Medical	50	35⅝	44¼	1/3
Wal-Mart	100	30⅞	42⅞	2/2
Zero	125	15¾	14½	4/3

June 1991

Oops. Ruth Huston, recording partner, read the minutes and they were corrected: Homer recommended VeriFone, not Veritone. Our portfolio's balance is down to $45,876.65, largely due to buying out Marilyn Ritter's share.

Maxine Thomas, junior partner, discussed two interesting articles, "Falling Interest Rates" from *Modern Maturity* and "Double Dip Recession" from *U.S. News & World Report.*

Stock Selection Committee member Ann Brewer reported on VeriFone, which makes devices used to verify credit card transactions. Their products are used by retailers, gas stations, convenience store operators, health care providers, and government agencies to electronically automate the processing of payments, benefits, and information transactions. She noted that the company is a leading-edge supplier, but that the supplier field is crowded with competitors. She concluded that it was a good company, but was concerned that the current price might be too high.

Doris Edwards reported on Gillette and concluded that, though it was a strong company and profits were expected to grow, at $38 per share, its price-earnings ratio was too high. Ann made a motion to purchase as many shares as possible of VeriFone, which was seconded by Doris. Motion carried.

Our next meeting date would fall on the Fourth of July, so Betty Sinnock suggested an evening at the Lake Wood Supper Club on July 18 instead.

Our Portfolio, 6/30/91

Stock	Number of shares	Purchase price per share	Current price	*Value Line's* timeliness / safety
A. G. Edwards	110	23	31¾	2/3
Archer Daniels Midland	105	24¼	23⅝	3/2
Baxter	100	21⅝	32¼	2/3
Calgon Carbon	50	21⅜	21	TK
CIPSCO	100	23¼	24⅝	3/1
Gannett	50	37⅜	41⅞	4/1
Glaxo Holdings	100	17⅞	40½	2/2
Hershey Foods	100	32¾	40¾	2/2
Lawter Intl.	133	9⅞	13	2/3
McDonald's	100	29⅜	32⅞	2/1
Rollins	100	16⅝	21⅛	2/3
RPM	200	10⅝	22¼	2/3
St. Jude Medical	50	35⅝	43½	1/3
VeriFone	100	18⅜	17¼	N.A.
Wal-Mart	100	30⅞	42¾	2/2

July 1991

We shared a delightful evening at the Lake Wood Supper Club. Twelve members and three guests from an investment club in Bloomington, Illinois, enjoyed a delicious meal. We then adjourned to a different room, where an informal meeting was held.

Betty Sinnock gave the financial report. Our portfolio has dropped to $44,915.08, due to drops in the price of Archer Daniels Midland, Baxter, CIPSCO, Lawter, Rollins, and St. Jude. Our cash balances are: First State Bank—$74.45; A. G. Edwards—$31.75.

Betty answered many questions from our guests, such as how we conduct our meetings and what steps we take when we look for a stock or industry to study. She told them that we use the latest summary from *Value Line* to find industries rated in the top 25 or 30 and then we use it to find the better growth companies in that industry.

No investment decisions were made.

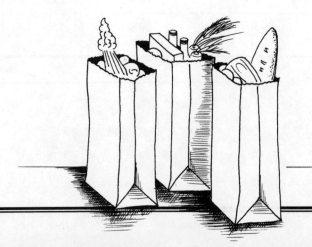

Our Portfolio, 7/31/91

Stock	Number of shares	Purchase price per share	Current price	*Value Line's* timeliness / safety
A. G. Edwards	165	15¼	25⅜	2/3
Archer Daniels Midland	105	23¾	25	3/2
Baxter	100	21⅝	34⅝	2/3
Calgon Carbon	50	21⅜	22⅜	3/3
CIPSCO	100	23¼	25	3/1
Gannett	100	37⅞	44¼	4/1
Glaxo Holdings	100	17⅞	44	2/2
Hershey Foods	100	32¾	41⅞	2/2
Lawter Intl.	133	9⅞	14¾	2/3
McDonald's	100	29⅜	32¾	2/1
Rollins	100	16⅝	25½	2/3
RPM	200	10⅝	21¾	2/3
St. Jude Medical	50	35⅝	50¾	2/3
VeriFone	100	18⅜	17⅝	N.A.
Wal-Mart	100	30⅞	47⅝	1/2

August 1991

We returned to Hardee's. Betty Sinnock gave the financial report: Our portfolio value is up to $48,320.18. Our cash balances are: First State Bank—$148.70; A. G. Edwards—$141.60.

Ruth Huston read a thank-you note from Shirley Gross for flowers sent to her while she was in the hospital. Maxine Thomas, junior partner, discussed two articles from *The Wall Street Journal*: "Deciding What to Buy and When to Sell" and "Investment Clubs Find New Popularity."

Stock Selection Committee member Ann Corley reported on Community Psych but didn't recommend it. Lillian Ellis reported on PepsiCo. She was very enthusiastic because the company owns three major restaurant chains—Pizza Hut, Kentucky Fried Chicken, and Taco Bell—as well as Frito Lay, the snack food company. After discussion, Shirley made a motion to sell Gannett, whose *Value Line* timeliness rating dropped to 4, and whose national newspaper, *USA Today*, is still not profitable, and buy 100 shares of PepsiCo. Ann Corley seconded and the motion carried.

Our Portfolio, 8/30/91

Stock	Number of shares	Purchase price per share	Current price	*Value Line's* timeliness / safety
A. G. Edwards	165	15¼	25⅞	2/3
Archer Daniels Midland	105	23¾	25¾	3/2
Baxter	100	21⅝	35⅝	2/3
Calgon Carbon	50	21⅜	23½	3/3
CIPSCO	100	23¼	25¼	3/1
Glaxo Holdings	100	17⅞	46¼	2/2
Hershey Foods	100	32¾	41⅞	3/2
Lawter Intl.	133	9⅞	14¾	2/3
McDonald's	100	29⅜	32⅝	2/1
PepsiCo	100	32⅞	32⅜	2/2
Rollins	100	16⅝	25⅝	2/3
RPM	200	10⅝	21½	2/3
St. Jude Medical	50	35⅝	52	2/3
VeriFone	100	18⅜	16¼	N.A.
Wal-Mart	100	30⅞	50⅝	1/2

September 1991

Our portfolio's value has risen to $49,077.96. Our cash on hand totals $1,919.20.

The club received many compliments on our television appearance, which aired on CBS on September 4 at 7:15 A.M. We will write to Arlene Bley to thank her for putting a cable connection for a television and a VCR in the Park House so we could watch the show at the continental breakfast after the taping.

Final plans were made for those attending the Heart of Illinois Fair in Peoria on September 28. Maxine Thomas, junior partner, reported on *U.S. News & World Report*'s "Untold Treasuries" story. A nominating committee for new officers was selected.

Helen Kramer reported on Lincoln National, where Carnell Korsmeyer's son-in-law works. Betty Sinnock passed out copies of a stock sheet on which she compared it to Crawford & Co. and American Bankers, which, at $49.75 a share, we can't afford. After discussion, Elsie Scheer made a motion to buy another 50 shares of Calgon Carbon, which had been written up in *Better Investing*. We like the stock because the company produces carbon used to purify drinking water, something we felt was really needed. Seconded by Doris Edwards, the motion carried.

Our Portfolio, 9/30/91

Stock	Number of shares	Purchase price per share	Current price	*Value Line's* timeliness / safety
A. G. Edwards	165	15¼	31⅛	1/3
Archer Daniels Midland	110	22⅝	25⅝	3/2
Baxter	100	21⅝	33⅝	2/3
Calgon Carbon	100	22¾	21½	3/3
CIPSCO	100	23¼	26½	3/1
Glaxo Holdings	100	17⅞	49	2/2
Hershey Foods	100	32¾	38⅞	3/2
Lawter Intl.	133	9⅞	15⅛	2/3
McDonald's	100	29⅜	35	3/1
PepsiCo	100	32⅞	28½	2/2
Rollins	100	16⅝	23⅞	2/3
RPM	200	10⅝	20¼	2/3
St. Jude Medical	50	35⅝	52	2/3
VeriFone	100	18⅜	18¾	N.A.
Wal-Mart	100	30⅞	47¾	1/2

October 1991

We met at Hardee's again and our portfolio's value is up to $50,517.45. We have lots of cash on hand—$1,269.95.

The slate of new officers was presented: senior partner Carnell Korsmeyer; junior partner Maxine Thomas; recording partner, Margaret Houchins; financial partner Betty Sinnock; social committee, Ruth Huston and Doris Edwards. Helen Kramer moved to accept and it was unanimous.

We discussed an article from *The Wall Street Journal*, "Investment Errors and How to Avoid Them."

Stock Selection Committee Member Hazel Lindahl reported on Casey's General Stores and Smithfield Foods, a pork producer. After much discussion, and since we had a partner associated with the pork industry, we considered investing in Smithfield Foods. Hazel was interested in Casey's because they had just opened two Casey's in Beardstown. We liked their chicken dinners and they seemed to be doing a good business. Carnell made a motion to buy 100 shares of Casey, but after the group discussion withdrew the motion. Ann Brewer made a motion to wait until next month to buy, Doris Edwards seconded it, and the motion carried.

Our Portfolio, 10/31/91

Stock	Number of shares	Purchase price per share	Current price	*Value Line's* timeliness/ safety
A. G. Edwards	110	15¼	33½	1/3
Archer Daniels Midland	105	22⅝	27⅜	2/2
Baxter	100	21⅝	37½	2/3
Calgon Carbon	25	22¾	21⅛	3/3
CIPSCO	100	23⅜	27⅛	3/1
Glaxo Holdings	100	17⅞	55½	2/2
Hershey Foods	100	32¾	41¼	2/2
Lawter Intl.	133	9⅞	14⅞	2/3
McDonald's	100	29⅜	34¾	3/1
PepsiCo	100	32⅞	28½	2/2
Rollins	100	16⅝	23⅝	2/3
RPM	200	10⅝	19¼	2/3
St. Jude Medical	50	35⅝	47½	2/3
VeriFone	100	18⅜	20	N.A.
Wal-Mart	100	30⅞	46¼	1/2

November 1991

Senior partner Carnell Korsmeyer opened the meeting at Hardee's. Our balances are: First State Bank—$1,388.53; A. G. Edwards—$357.36. Our portfolio's value has climbed to $51,935.89.

Stock Selection Committee member Carnell Korsmeyer reported on Smithfield Foods and we decided to buy 100 shares because the upside-down ratio was better than last month. After discussion, Maxine made a motion to buy another 50 shares of St. Jude, seconded by Elsie Scheer. The motion didn't pass because we felt that the current price was too high.

Our next meeting will be a Christmas party at Lake Wood Supper Club.

Our Portfolio, 11/30/91

Stock	Number of shares	Purchase price per share	Current price	*Value Line's* timeliness/ safety
A. G. Edwards	165	15¼	29¼	1/3
Archer Daniels Midland	110	22⅝	27⅜	2/2
Baxter	100	21⅝	36⅜	2/3
Calgon Carbon	100	22¾	19⅞	3/3
CIPSCO	100	22¼	26⅞	3/1
Glaxo Holdings	200	8⅞	27¼	2/2
Hershey Foods	100	32¾	38	1/2
Lawter Intl.	133	9⅞	15⅜	2/3
McDonald's	100	29⅜	33⅝	1
PepsiCo	100	32⅞	29⅝	2/2
Rollins	100	16⅝	24⅜	2/3
RPM	200	10⅝	19	3/3
Smithfield Foods	100	21	17	2/3
St. Jude Medical	50	35⅝	47¾	2/3
VeriFone	100	18⅜	18¼	N.A.
Wal-Mart	100	30⅞	48⅞	1/2

December 1991

We had no formal meeting, but Betty announced at our Christmas party that our portfolio was valued at $52,152.90.

January 1992

Betty did the final calculations for our performance last year. We were very proud to achieve a 54.04% return, our best ever! And better yet, we had a 59½% return on the stocks that traded on the New York Stock Exchange!

Our Portfolio, 12/31/91

Stock	Number of shares	Purchase price per share	Current price	*Value Line's* timeliness / safety
A. G. Edwards	165	15¼	37⅞	1/3
Archer Daniels Midland	110	22⅝	33⅛	2/2
Baxter Travenol	100	21⅝	40	2/3
Calgon Carbon	100	22¾	21⅜	3/3
CIPSCO	100	23¼	27⅞	3/1
Glaxo Holdings	200	8⅞	31¾	2/2
Hershey Foods	100	32¾	44⅜	2/2
Lawter Intl.	177	7⅜	13½	2/3
McDonald's	100	29⅜	38	2/1
PepsiCo	100	32⅞	33⅞	2/2
Rollins	100	16⅝	28⅝	2/3
RPM	200	10⅝	23⅛	3/3
Smithfield Foods	100	21	16¾	3/3
St. Jude Medical	50	35⅝	55½	2/3
VeriFone	100	18⅜	18⅛	N.A.
Wal-Mart	100	30⅞	58⅞	2/2

19. Rewards of Investing: What We Spend Our Money On

If you want to read about wild spending habits, you'd better buy another book. We haven't spent a dime of the money we have made in the club, except to add to our portfolio. During our first 10 years together, none of our members has made withdrawals on their accounts.

Many of the Ladies have built up personal portfolios outside the club, however, and everyone uses what they learn at meetings to manage their money. Individually, our members have invested in certificates of deposit (CDs), Treasury bonds and notes, mutual funds, annuities, and individual stocks. The money they have made has helped them do everything from redecorate their homes to cruise to Greece.

"I always pay myself first, before I pay a single bill," says

Ann Brewer, who sets aside $300 every month to invest in several stocks through NAIC's Low-Cost Reinvestment Plan. Margaret Houchins, who is also buying stocks through NAIC's program, invested in McDonald's after she studied the company with the club.

RPM was the first stock that Ruth Huston, who inherited some shares in a local bank, Farmers Elevator, and CIPSCO, bought for herself. She says she liked the company from the moment she learned about it at a club meeting. "They have 46 years of consecutive record earnings," she boasts. "When I can afford it, I'm going to invest more. There are lots of things I would like to buy, including Mobil Oil stock and gold." Doris Edwards added a couple of stocks that the club studied to her assets, which include an annuity, bonds, and savings accounts. She enjoys spending money on family members, especially her nieces and nephews, and travel.

Helen Kramer has a small personal portfolio, including stocks, mutual funds, and an annuity. She uses the money to keep up her home and her car and to take day trips.

Shirley Gross, our most experienced investor, has built up her portfolio over 18 years. Sometimes she buys what the club buys. Like Margaret, she added McDonald's to her portfolio when the club invested in it.

When Shirley bought her house, she simply sold some of her stocks and paid cash. It is a handsome, sprawling ranch with a studio for her painting, where we often have our meetings. Shirley has also used income from her investments to help send her five grandchildren to college.

Maxine Thomas and Lillian Ellis, who both have personal portfolios, have used their money to travel around the world, often as roommates. "I love to travel. I have my little file and keep track of my investments and see how they are doing," says Maxine. "If I have a trip that I would like to take, I'll see which ones that I want to take the interest from."

Maxine and Lillian have traveled to England, Ireland, and Scotland; toured Alaska by cruise ship, train, and bus; and explored Australia and New Zealand and the Mediterranean. Most recently they ventured to Israel and Egypt for a 15-day tour of the Holy Land.

"I am cautious about what I do with my money," says Lillian. "I try to use it in the best way that I can. I have a small portfolio of my own and I have income from that. I own CDs and am just getting into mutual funds. You have to stay on top of them all the time." Lillian, who also owns a building with four apartments in it, rents out three and lives in one. "I've been redecorating it each year, room by room, and getting it the way I want it, comfortable."

Betty Sinnock, our financial partner, didn't start investing in securities until four years ago. Now she has 11 stocks in a self-directed IRA, a 401K pension plan invested in a common stock fund, an international equity mutual fund, and a few individual stocks.

Some members steer clear of the market or stick with investments they made before they joined the club. Sylvia Gaushell keeps her money in CDs and savings accounts, as does Hazel Lindahl. Ann Corley continues to hold on to Merck and Glaxo, which she bought with her husband since she joined the club. Buffy Tillitt-Pratt bought several stocks, including Wal-Mart, Merck, and Cifra, before she joined the club but has not bought any since. "I sat on Cifra for one and a half years," she muses, "then the club bought it and it went way up."

Elsie Scheer inherited money when her husband died in 1978. "I kept it in the bank mostly," she says. She now invests primarily in mutual funds, annuities, and CDs. Her daughter, Carol McCombs, who recently joined the club, is restricting her investments to her $25 monthly dues for a while.

"Farmers traditionally invest in their own business," confesses Carnell Korsmeyer. "The saying is that if they won a million dollars in the lottery, they'd just keep farming until it was gone." But Carnell and her husband, who own a hog farm, have also begun to invest in the stock market. Like several other members of the club, Carnell consults a financial adviser and feels more confident when she talks with him because of her experience in the club. "We like understanding what is being done, so we are not as vulnerable."

20. Profiles and Recipes

Ann Brewer

Since I was born in 1933 during the Depression, it was drilled into me to save for a "rainy day," not to take any chances with my money, and not to go into debt except to purchase a home. I didn't explore other avenues of making money work for me as a young person.

I graduated from Beardstown High School and was hired by the Beardstown Board of Education as a secretary when I was 17. I have been there ever since. I've enjoyed working and hope to continue until it ceases to be fun. Who wants to go home and dust?

My husband and I are the parents of two grown children who now live out of state. I tried to stress to our children that if you don't pay yourself first, whether it be $5, $10, $50, $100, or $500, then your money has a way of disappearing. I have encouraged them to invest in the stock market and given them subscriptions to NAIC publications.

The members in our club are very close. Recently my husband had surgery and I spent a lot of time with him in the hospital. We had a nice card from the Ladies with a note saying, "Our prayers and our thoughts are with you. If you need anything, please give us a call." I think that says it all.

I feel that women need to gain financial information— whether they be young, middle-aged, or old. If they have to manage their own affairs, they will need to be knowledgeable. It's always helpful to have assistance from your broker, banker, and attorney, but the bottom line is that you have to make the decisions and not rely on others.

Ann's Kentucky Cream Cake

½ cup shortening
1 stick margarine
2 cups sugar
5 egg yolks
2 cups cake flour or
   2¼ cups all-purpose
   flour

1 tsp. baking soda
1 cup buttermilk
1 tsp. vanilla
1 cup coconut
⅔ cup chopped nuts
5 egg whites, beaten

FROSTING

8 oz. cream cheese
1 stick margarine
1½ lbs. powdered sugar

1 tsp. vanilla
½ cup chopped nuts

Cream shortening and margarine with sugar. Add egg yolks one at a time. Beat well. Add flour and soda alternately with buttermilk. Add vanilla, coconut, and nuts. Fold in beaten egg whites. Pour mixture into 3 9-inch-round pans or 1 9 × 13″ pan. Bake at 350 degrees for 25 to 30 minutes.

For frosting, cream first four ingredients, frost cake, then sprinkle nuts on top.

Ann Corley

Pana, a small town near Springfield, is where I grew up. After high school I studied stenography and was offered a job with good pay in Springfield, where I met my husband, Donald, at a dance. He flashed his pearly whites at me and I flashed mine back.

In the early years of our marriage, my husband invested in the stock market. I knew very little about stocks or the stock market and was not interested at the time. His work required him to travel a lot and I was busy raising our three sons. He kept me informed as to what he was buying or selling and the cost.

One evening at dinner he mentioned a stock that he was interested in and said, "I'm going to buy 100 shares." This puzzled our three-year-old son, who asked, "Daddy, why are you going to buy so many chairs?"

We moved several times within Illinois as my husband pursued a career in banking. When he retired in 1981, he

was president of First National Bank in Beardstown.

Donald talked to Shirley, and Betty, who was an employee of the bank at that time, about the club and was very impressed. At his suggestion, I joined the club in 1985. I joined when a member withdrew from the partnership; I bought out her share for $624.49. Today my investment, including monthly contributions, is worth more than 10 times that.

I watch CNN's "Nightly Business Report" and "Crossfire." I like to know what's going on in the world and how it will affect the stock market. I subscribe to The Wall Street Journal *and* Investor's Business Daily.

Since my husband's death in July 1993, I have had to make all my own investment decisions. I am really glad I joined this club and learned as much as I have.

Ann's Sour Cream Noodle Bake

When I bring this dish to a potluck,
everyone wants the recipe.

NOODLE MIXTURE
1 8-oz. pkg. noodles
1 Tbs. cooking oil
1 cup cottage cheese
1 cup sour cream
½ cup chopped green onion

BEEF MIXTURE
¼ tsp. garlic salt
1 large can tomato sauce
1 lb. ground beef
   (browned)

Boil the noodles (follow package instructions) and add cooking oil to water when noodles are nearly done. Drain. In a 9 × 13 pan, alternate layers of noodle mixture with beef mixture. Top with shredded sharp cheese. Bake at 350 degrees for 30 minutes.

Doris Edwards

Currently a principal at Gard Elementary School, I have been a principal in Beardstown since 1959.

I grew up on a farm near Macomb in west-central Illinois with my parents, three sisters, and three brothers. We walked to the big red schoolhouse on the hill every day with our classmates.

After graduation and two years of study at Western Illinois State Teachers College, I started teaching in a country school near Sciota, 11 miles from my home, in 1939. Having attended a rural school, I knew what my work would be. I had to teach all subjects in grades one through eight. We had 52 classes a day with 16 students ranging from five to 16 years of age. Teachers in country schools did the janitorial work, cleaned the chalkboards, fired the furnace, and went to the pump in the yard for water. We had outside toilets, the whole bit.

Everyone brought their lunch. During my third year at this school, the hot lunch program was started. Surplus commodities were brought to us and we got a hotplate to cook on. Before that we'd warm our soup or other foods on top of the furnace.

After three years, there was only one student residing in the district. He and I moved down the road two miles to the next district, where I remained for five years until that district consolidated with the other country schools and we were moved into Sciota. That student, who had studied with me for eight years, went on to high school and is now one of the directors of the largest bank in Macomb.

With the closing of the country schools, I went to Pekin and taught second grade for five years before coming to Beardstown in 1951. During my first years of teaching, I continued my work toward a bachelor's degree by going to school during the summers, evenings, and Saturdays. After

I moved to Beardstown, I resumed my studies toward the master's degree while teaching full-time.

Even though we lived on a farm and had a garden as well as our own cows, pigs, and chickens, my father was a civil engineer. He was the County Superintendent of Highways, and through the Depression, with the help of WPA workers, he resurfaced all of the county roads and built many bridges. My folks paid for my first two years of college; I paid for the remainder of my education. Going to school, paying rent, buying textbooks, clothes, and so forth, I didn't have the money or the time to think about investing.

When I was teaching in the rural schools, I would discuss investments, stocks and bonds. During World War II, I bought war bonds, but I never felt I had the money to invest in stocks. The first year I started teaching I was the third highest paid teacher in the county, with a salary of $90 a month. The next year I received a monthly increase of $2.50 and thought that was great.

There is so much I don't know about investing; membership in the club for me is a learning situation. As we listened to the presentation about making a video on investing, I could sense that some of our members were very hesitant; all I heard were no's. When my turn came to voice an opinion, I said, "I guess it is the teacher coming out in me, but I feel that if we can do anything to help educate other people that there is a way to make money by doing wise investing, we should make the video. It could be used as a teaching tool." The nearer I come to retirement, the more I say, "I wish I had started investing years ago."

Doris's Four-Bean Salad

1 can kidney beans, drained	1 can lima beans, drained
1 can wax beans, drained	½ cup green peppers, chopped
1 can green beans, drained	1 onion, chopped

DRESSING

½ cup vinegar	½ cup salad oil
½ cup sugar	salt & pepper to taste

Mix dressing ingredients and pour over vegetables. Refrigerate overnight.

Lillian Ellis

My husband was interested in stocks and I picked it up after we were married. I read The Wall Street Journal *and the various business magazines we subscribed to. We had a small portfolio, but I look back now and see we really didn't know what we were doing. I wish I could have been in this club before. We'd look at a stock and buy it and if it didn't perform right, we'd sell it. You just can't do that. You've got to hold them and I know that now.*

After he passed away, I was kind of let down. I gave up on stocks until the opportunity came along with the Business and Professional Women's Club. I was probably the first one at the meeting. I thought, "Now this is what I want. I want to learn, and I need this because I need to get out and be among people."

The most important thing I've learned is to manage my money. I needed to buckle down to make my money work for me. I am more cautious and I try to use it in the best way I can. I have income from a small portfolio, for instance, that needs to be handled properly and other money coming in that needs to be budgeted.

I am getting into mutual funds now on my own. You have to look at all these things and stay on top of them all the time.

I have been following Glaxo ever since the club bought it because I found it very interesting. They are constantly bringing up new drugs and are working all the time. Invest in something that you are interested in and you will follow it. In fact, the first thing I look at in the paper in the morning is Glaxo, and then I look at the stock I am following for the club. Right now the drug stocks are very interesting because of all this controversy with Wal-Mart and Osco selling their drugs at cut rates. It makes for compelling reading.

I was born in Beardstown and my father worked on the railroad maintaining big steam locomotives. My mother passed away when my sister and I, who are 11 months apart, were quite young. I was three. My dad raised us with my grandmother and an assortment of aunts.

We graduated from high school during the Depression and my dad was out of work. I know what it means to stretch money, to make money go a long way. I would not have changed my life for anything in the world. When I look back, goodness, that was about the best training anyone could ever have.

After high school I went to work at Woolworth's. I was very shy and that helped me to meet people. Then I did government work during the war, inspecting government gloves in a glove factory. I made real good money, which was important because we really needed it.

Then the dentist who had done my dental work since I was a small child asked me to come work for him as his assistant. He had noticed that whenever I went for an appointment I'd ask many questions, so he trained me. That was the work I loved. Twenty-three years and I loved every minute of it. If you can get a job like that, you've got it made.

Later, when his wife died, I married him. He was a wonderful person. He died 17 years ago, but I have three stepchildren, step-grandchildren, step great-grandchildren, so I am blessed.

I'm 77. I can pretty much do what I want to do. I take care of everything in the building that I live in. I have four apartments; I rent three and I live in one. It keeps me busy.

Lillian's Chicken Supreme

1 boned, cooked chicken, diced
1 7-oz. package Creamettes (do not cook)
1 pint milk
2 cans mushroom or cream of chicken soup
1 small onion (cut fine)
½ lb. Velveeta cheese (cut in ½-inch cubes)
4 hard-cooked eggs (cut up)

Mix together all the ingredients, but reserve 1 cup milk. Let stand overnight in refrigerator. Take out 1 hour before you bake it. Add 1 cup milk. Bake for 1 hour at 350 degrees in a 9 × 13 pan.

Sylvia Gaushell

I joined the club two or three years ago at the suggestion of my friend, Ann Brewer. I never knew much about stocks before I joined, but I do now. I think the club meetings are all real interesting. I don't know how to figure out all the ratios, but I'm working on it.

I'm a retired schoolteacher; I used to be an arts supervisor. I enjoy using pastel, watercolor, oils, and acrylic paints. I also make quilts.

I grew up and taught in Quincy, Illinois. My husband and I moved to Beardstown in 1935. We have a son and a daughter.

I enjoy being in a club with people that I know; there is an element of trust. I take the Chicago Tribune *and look up the stocks every day. If I see articles about the companies that we are studying, I cut them out and send them to the members.*

I follow Merck for the club. I'd never heard of it before. It has gone down a little, but I still think it's a good stock because the demand is there for prescription medicines.

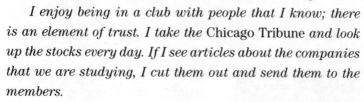

Sylvia's Beef Stew

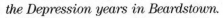

1 lb. stewing beef, cubed	2 cups water with 2 tbs. corn
4 large carrots, sliced	starch blended in
4 to 6 potatoes, cubed	1 large can tomatoes with
1 large onion, diced	juice
1 stalk celery, diced	1 Tbs. kitchen bouquet
	salt and pepper to taste

Combine all ingredients in a large covered pan and bake at 350 degrees for 3 to 4 hours.

Shirley Gross

When I was born in 1917, my father worked for the railroad. Later my mother ran a small grocery store and put my father through law school. My brother and I grew up during the Depression years in Beardstown.

After graduating from high school I went to Stephens College in Columbia, Missouri, for two years and then completed a B.A. degree in chemistry at Illinois College in Jacksonville.

I interned for a year at St. John's Hospital in Springfield and received a degree in medical technology. I worked there three years and then got married and moved to Springfield. At that time it was difficult to get hired if you were married, but I found part-time work. I also had two children, David, who is now a geologist, and Susan, a special education teacher.

In 1957, I moved back to Beardstown. I worked at Beardstown Hospital as a technician for seven years. After that I worked as assistant librarian at the Beardstown Public Library for seven years before retiring.

I started painting in the late 1960's. I had always wanted to do it, but didn't have time when I was working and raising a family. I started investing in 1974 or 1975. My primary income is from farming. My brother and I invested in farmland in Beardstown when it was selling quite cheaply in the early 1960s. We grow beans and corn and sometimes wheat.

I'm a director of First State Bank in Beardstown, a trustee of First Congregational Church in Beardstown, and a trustee of Beardstown Public Library.

Shirley's Stock Market Muffins
(Guaranteed to rise!)

MIX BY HAND:
7½ oz. POST Raisin Bran
   (4 cups)
1½ cups sugar
2½ cups flour
2½ teaspoons baking soda
1 tsp. salt

ADD:
1 stick melted margarine
2 eggs
2 cups buttermilk

Refrigerate for a few days before baking. Bake in muffin tins at 400 degrees for 15 to 20 minutes. Keep the rest of dough tightly covered in the refrigerator and it will last for 5 weeks.

Margaret Houchins

I run the Countryside Florist and Gift Shop on Wall Street in Beardstown. I work six days a week and my daughter helps me.

I've been a member of the club for three years. Betty Sinnock came to BPW and gave a program that night and introduced me for the first time to the investment club. I had heard the term before, but I thought that it was always for rich people.

I was always interested in Wall Street and buying stocks, I guess because I wanted to be financially independent. But I thought that unless you have thousands and thousands of dollars you just can't get involved.

I was born and raised in Kansas City in the 1940s. My parents both worked in an airplane factory at the time. My parents were real conservative and never willing to take a risk. They were very happy with 3 or 4 or 5% interest on their money because it was very secure to them. Maybe because I grew up in a different generation I am willing to take more of a risk.

I am in the reinvestment program through the NAIC and I highly recommend it. For a person who doesn't have a lot of money to invest, who just wants to invest a little bit every month, they can do it through the low-cost investment program. There's no broker's fees and you can send a set amount every month to add to your investments. They give you an accounting and you can watch it grow and you can buy more or sell anytime you want. It's another learning experience because you're going to keep track of that stock that you are buying and you know personally you're in control of it.

I got married right after I left high school and was married for 21 years and then my husband left. I didn't work while I was married, so I was thrown into the work

force with no skills and four daugh-
ters. I worked two jobs trying to put
my daughter Vicki through college.
I worked for a savings and loan as
a data processor and then I cleaned
offices at night.

I had been friends with Jerry for
years before we decided to get mar-
ried. We've been married for nine
years and we raise and show horses.
I have a Missouri Foxtrotter.

I am president of the St. Luke's
Auxiliary, so I knew a lot of the
women in the club that way.

People are moving into smaller,
rural communities because there is that friendliness. My
husband and I go to lunch every day together. When we
walk down the street, we are just continuously waving. It's
a good feeling, it really is.

Margaret's Even-Bush-Would-Like-It
Broccoli Casserole

6 eggs	1 pkg. frozen or 1 cup fresh
6 Tbs. flour	chopped broccoli
½ stick margarine	2 cups shredded cheddar
Large carton of small curd	cheese
cottage cheese	Optional: 1 green onion,
	chopped

Beat eggs. Add flour a tablespoon at a time while beating.
Then add chunks of margarine. Fold in cottage cheese. Thaw
broccoli by placing in colander and running hot water over
it. Add to mixture. Add cheese. Pour into a greased open
casserole dish and bake at 350 degrees for 1 hour.

Ruth Huston

I grew up on a farm three and a half miles east of Beards-town in Sangamon Valley, where we experienced many floods. I moved to town after graduating from Beardstown High School in 1936 and worked at Wells Lamont Glove Factory for eight and a half years.

My husband, Norman, was among the first group of married men inducted into service from Cass County in 1942, and he served in Europe until 1945. After he returned home, we opened our own dry-cleaning plant, which we operated for 26 years. I worked side by side with him except for five years when we were raising our adopted son, Dale. I stayed home until Dale started school. After my husband's death in 1972, I sold the shop. I have worked part time as a secretary and volunteer at church and delivering Meals on Wheels.

As I was growing up, I watched my cousin become a very successful broker. I really looked up to him because he

had done so well, but back then I didn't have any money to invest. Later in life I inherited several stocks and when the dividend checks came in at Christmastime, I did my shopping. One stock was Farmer's Elevator and they had done some remodeling one year. When no check came, was I disappointed! When the opportunity came to join the investment club, I jumped at the chance.

I've really enjoyed the club. I have known a few of the members for a long time and others I didn't know until the club was formed. We have become very close friends and I love each of them in a special way.

It's exciting to have been on national television and in the papers. We always have fun at our photo sessions. Friends and other people tease us, asking for autographs and also for stock tips. But we have no secrets.

Ruth's 5-Hour Stew

3 carrots	2 Tbs. tapioca
3 potatoes	1 can beef broth
2 celery stalks	Salt and pepper to taste
½ onion	
1 pound stewing beef, cubed	

Slice, dice, or cube the vegetables. Place all ingredients in a roaster pan. Mix and cover. Bake 5 hours at 250 degrees. Do not open the oven or peek at the stew while it is baking!

Carnell Korsmeyer

During our entire married life my husband and I, as farmers and pork producers, have invested and reinvested in our own business. Farmers traditionally invest in their own business. The saying is, "If they won $1 million in the lottery, they'd just keep farming until it was gone."

My husband farmed with his brother until 1968, when we split and went into the hog business. I didn't do much hands-on with the hogs. We had employees, so I did the office, payroll, and things.

Our four children have all chosen careers other than farming, so they are not coming back to take over. It seemed prudent to learn other forms of investment as retirement approaches.

When the group of BPW members expressed an interest in forming an investment club, which offered a steady, applied, low-cost method of learning, it was consistent with our lifelong practice of investing in business. It also answers a personal sense of needing to be part of a larger picture.

I believe in the free enterprise system. In order for that to work, it takes money. If you invest in that, you are part of a bigger world. It's also somewhat risky but it's a steady, calculated risk with positive results.

We visited Russia last year and that brought all this home very graphically and plainly. We were on a People-to-People tour and we were put in touch with people who were interested in farming, including collective and state farm people. Some groups were interested in privatizing.

We learned how difficult that is when there's no historical precedent for it. We take a lot for granted here in having privatized business as part of our way of life.

I was born in Beardstown in 1927 and grew up here. My father was an agent for a gas company and my mother was a homemaker. I studied nursing for a short time, then worked at the Central Illinois Public Service Co. until I was married.

My husband and I have served on several boards and committees for the pork industry. In 1992 I was appointed to the National Pork Board by the Secretary of Agriculture. It was a great honor to be recommended by my peers.

Carnell's Favorite Ham Loaf
(Courtesy of the National Pork Producers' Association)

2 lbs. ground ham
1 lb. ground lean pork
4 eggs
2½ cups soft breadcrumbs
1½ cups milk
½ cup brown sugar
4 tsp. prepared mustard
½ tsp. pepper

TOPPING
1 cup brown sugar
1 Tbs. corn starch
¼ tsp. salt
8½ oz. canned crushed pineapple
2 Tbs. lemon juice
1 Tbs. mustard

Mix ingredients thoroughly and shape into 10 to 12 individual loaves. Place in open baking dish.

Prepare topping by mixing ingredients and cooking over heat until the mixture thickens. Let cool. Pour ⅔ of topping over ham loaves. Bake at 350 degrees for 1 to 1½ hours, basting periodically with remaining topping.

Helen Kramer

Being a member of the Beardstown Business and Professional Women's Investment Club is one of the best things that could have happened to me. I joined the club because I was a widow and was aware that it was my responsibility to take care of my money and invest it profitably for personal gain.

Words cannot express what this club means to me. The #1 goal, "Learn," has been a tremendous help to me in investing. We take investing seriously, but not so seriously as not to meet goal #2, "Have fun," along the way by having dinner meetings and visiting our stockbroker's office and the Board of Trade in Chicago. Figures prove that we are reaching goal #3, "Make money."

Being a member of BWP Investment Club has really changed my life and broadened my horizons. I have met many outstanding people and made many friends across the country. Being a member of NAIC and recording secretary of the Heart of Illinois Investment Council has kept me very busy and informed about NAIC, which is basically an educational organization whose principal job is to help members learn more about sound stock selection procedures.

My favorite stock at this time is Hershey Foods. I can relate to the company because I toured the factory in Hershey, Pennsylvania, and saw how many different candies were made and also sampled some. Hershey Foods is the largest public U.S. producer of chocolate and confectionery products. They also make pasta.

I was born on a farm near Beardstown, the oldest of four children. I attended Beardstown schools and graduated from Beardstown High School during the Depression days, when jobs were hard to find. I was fortunate to get a job at the First State Bank of Beardstown the fall after graduation and spent all my working years at the same bank. I was vice president when I retired after 50 years.

One of my former bank presidents told me when I was about to take another job that I might not make so much money at the bank but that I would have security. After 50 years, I know he was right.

My husband was a farmer and after his passing I moved into Beardstown. I have been active in the First United Methodist Church as secretary of the administrative council and treasurer of United Methodist Women. I am treasurer of two local drainage districts, Emblem Club treasurer, Tri-County Community Concerts secretary, and Bible Study class member, and do other volunteer work.

Helen's Springtime Pie

2 9-inch pie shells baked
   (follow instructions on
   package)
1 large or two small cans
   mandarin oranges
3 large bananas cut into
   pineapple chunk sizes

1 large can pineapple chunks
1 box orange tapioca pudding
1 box vanilla tapioca pudding
Cool Whip or whipped cream

Drain juice from pineapple and oranges, save, and add water to make three cups. Cook puddings using the juice and water. Pour into shells and cool. Stir in the fruit, making sure the bananas are covered, and let set overnight. Top with cream.

Hazel Lindahl

I was married in Chicago and lived there for 23 years. I worked as a medical technician at Illinois Research Hospital. Then we moved to my father's farm near Barry, Illinois, where my husband, Harry, raised Boston Terriers and Pointers. I was employed as a registered nurse at St. Mary's Hospital in Quincy, Illinois.

Next, we purchased a small acreage near Smithfield. Harry continued to raise dogs and I worked as a medical technician at Graham Hospital in Canton. Later, I was employed as a public health nurse.

Harry died in 1971. My sister asked me to "retire" and come to Beardstown to help care for our mother, who was suffering from Alzheimer's disease. In Beardstown, I worked for a while as a school nurse and later worked part time at the public library.

I am a charter member of the investment club and I feel the knowledge gleaned from the club has helped me understand and manage my personal finances much better.

Hazel's Quick-Return Meal
Truthfully, my favorite recipe:

Walk to the freezer cabinets in your favorite grocery store. Pick out a yummy-looking meal in a box. Take to checkout counter. Head for home and pop it in the microwave oven. Enjoy!

Carol McCombs

I learned about investing from my mother, who has been a member of the club since its beginning. She was always talking about different stocks they purchased as a club. I usually let it go in one ear and out the other, but then I got to thinking about investing. The club approach seems to be a great way to learn about stocks and have fun while you are doing it. Since you only meet once a month and don't buy and sell sporadically, it is a safe and relatively inexpensive way to get involved with the market.

Since I recently became a member I don't have a lot of knowledge about the market, but I'm learning. The process of studying a stock is very educational and very interesting. So far my life hasn't changed because of joining the club, but I feel that in the future I'd like to invest some on my own, as my finances permit and with the knowledge I've gained from the club.

My family is very supportive. My husband, Bill, works for a local utility company. We've been married for 24 years and live on the family farm next door to my mother and my brother. I've always worked in the business field. For 22 years I did clerical work for a local manufacturing company. When they left the area, that put me in the market for a job. I began working for an insurance agency here in town and became a licensed agent. My work is very challenging because we have to keep up with all the changes in the insurance world.

My husband and I have two children. My son, Marty, 23 years old, graduated from Lincoln College and

is employed by Brauer Pork. My daughter Cindy, 14, is a freshman in high school. She hopes to pursue a music career. Both kids were active in 4-H.

My husband is involved with the vfw *and Lion's Club. I'm on the County Extension Council and also involved with the Community Theatre Group.*

Carol's Hawaiian Sweet Bread

6½ cups all-purpose flour
¾ cup mashed potato flakes
⅔ cup sugar
1 tsp. salt
½ teaspoon ground ginger
2 tsp. pure vanilla
2 packages active dry yeast

1 cup milk
½ cup water
½ cup margarine
1 cup pineapple juice
    (at room temperature)
3 eggs

In a large bowl, combine 3 cups flour, potato flakes, sugar, salt, ginger, vanilla, and yeast. In medium saucepan, heat milk, water, and margarine until very warm (120 to 130 degrees). Add warm liquid, pineapple juice, and eggs to flour mixture. Blend with electric mixer at low speed until well moistened; beat at medium speed for 4 minutes.

By hand, stir in 3 cups of flour to form a stiff dough. On a floured surface, knead in ½ to 1 cup flour until smooth, about 5 minutes. Place dough in a greased bowl. Cover with clean towel. Let rise until doubled in size, about 90 minutes. Punch dough down.

This is very light dough and very tasty. It can be shaped into dinner rolls of any shape. I also use this dough to make cinnamon rolls (or you can use it to make bread). After shaping the dough into desired forms, let it rise until doubled in size. Bake dinner rolls for 15 to 20 minutes in a 350-degree oven (until browned).

Elsie Scheer

I may be just a retired farm wife, but life sure hasn't passed me by. Life gets more exciting year after year, especially since joining this investment club.

I was born and raised in Springfield, Illinois. During the Depression years, four-year college was out of the question for many of us, so I attended Brown's Business College.

Soon after graduating I, of all things, married a farmer and moved to Beardstown. Keeping farm records was the only way I used my education.

I soon learned many new things, such as cleaning chickens, canning, gardening, butchering, mowing big yards, driving a car, and raising a family. My husband, William, and I were blessed with two girls and a boy. In 1978, I became a widow and our son continued running the farm. With three homes very close together on this farm, we remain a close-knit family, with my daughter and son living nearby. Ten grandchildren and seven great-grandchildren have been added, and in 1994 there are to be two more weddings, so the family is sure growing.

Being a very active grandmother, my time has been spent doing church work and being a 4-H leader for over 30 years. I am still involved with 4-H and extension work because my youngest granddaughter now is in 4-H.

After my husband's death, I had the opportunity of being a teacher's aide for two years in our Lutheran school, which gave me the privilege of joining the Business and Professional Women's Club. When you be-

come widowed your lifestyle changes a great deal, and my good friend, Hazel, who is in the investment club, looked after my social life. When the BPW Investment Club was mentioned, she encouraged me to join, so I became one of the charter members in 1983.

Having hit the upper 70s, you need to keep your mind busy, so this club was a great opportunity for studying and learning. Not only do we get down to brass tacks and study, but we have fun meeting at different dining places. Our brainstorming through stock selections has brought us good gains in our portfolio over our 10 years. Even our broker, Homer Rieken, is very proud of us and has taken us out for a wonderful meal. After all we've been through, who wouldn't be on Cloud Nine? Our club holds never-ending surprises and we just keep rolling right along, wondering what will happen next.

A highlight for me has been having my youngest daughter taken into the club. I had mentioned to one of our partners that I would like for her to take over my portfolio if anything happened to me, so that put her on the waiting list. A partner cashed out, so Carol got to fill the spot.

Being a very active 4-H family, we became accustomed to taking entries to the Illinois State Fair. Even Grandma started entering white & chocolate angel food cakes. I earned first-place ribbons for many years, and still do.

I do all sorts of crafts and sewing. In 1970, I started making corn-husk dolls. Living on a farm, I could select choice husks and would gather around 400 ears each year, stripping off the husks and saving the silks for hair. I demonstrated making the dolls at Clayville for their Spring and Fall Craft Festivals, but had to give it up in 1990 because of back problems.

Getting up in years is no reason for having time on your hands. Even though I can't do some things, I still have plenty to keep me busy. Just can't wait for the mail to come so I can check the stock report in the newspaper. Studying and keeping abreast of our various stocks creates a lot of interest as each partner in the club has a certain stock to study, and report on at each meeting.

Elsie's Prize-Winning Angel Food Cake

1½ cups egg whites (use 12 large eggs)
1 cup powdered sugar
1 cup cake flour (sift powdered sugar and flour together five times)

1 cup granulated sugar
½ tsp. salt
1 tsp. cream of tartar
1 tsp. vanilla
⅛ tsp. almond extract

Beat egg whites on high speed with salt. Add cream of tartar when foamy. Gradually add granulated sugar a small amount at a time when whites form soft peaks and continue beating until stiff. Fold in flavorings. Fold in flour and powdered sugar and put in a 10-inch tube pan. Bake at 425 degrees for 15 minutes, then turn oven back to 375 degrees and bake 15 minutes longer. Invert pan to cool and remove cake.

For Chocolate Angel Food Cake: Substitute ¼ cup cocoa for a little of the flour.

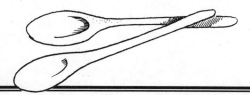

Betty Sinnock

I was born in Dayton, Ohio, but my folks moved back to Rushville, Illinois, when I was six. I went to school there and attended Western Illinois University, where I studied to be an elementary school teacher. I left to be married before I got my degree, thinking that I wanted to have my family early and once my children were old enough to go to school, I would be able to teach. At that time in Illinois, you didn't need a degree to teach.

When our youngest daughter was in school and I was ready to look for a teaching position, I found out that they changed the law and you had to have a degree. One day, when I was in a grocery store which a friend managed and he was lamenting that he didn't have any help, I suggested that I could be a cashier. He gave me a $20 bill and asked me to make change; he wanted to know how accurate I was and then how quickly I could start. Because I was somebody he could trust, he taught me how to do the books and the bank deposits.

I had worked there about a year and a half when the manager took his family on vacation for a month to California and I then had to spend 50, maybe 60 hours a week doing what I had to do for the store. In the meantime, my husband had gotten a much better job and I really didn't think I needed to work. So one day when I was in the bank making the deposit for the store, I mentioned that as soon as the boss got back I was going to turn in my resignation.

That night I got a telephone call asking if I would like to work at the bank. The hours would be much fewer. So in 1966 I went in as a teller. Later I was promoted to customer service, where I was at the time the investment club was mentioned. I would wonder at work when I heard people talking about their portfolio what it was. To me, it was a briefcase.

I always enjoyed math. The bank sent me to some classes in Springfield and I was promoted to the Trust Department as a trust officer. Later I switched to the trust department of the Havana National Bank. I have studied investments in week-long seminars at Notre Dame's Cannon School of Finance and in financial planning courses.

In 1993, I was elected to NAIC's national board of directors. I spend much of my free time giving talks to other investment clubs because I enjoy teaching others what I have learned.

My husband worked at the Oscar Mayer plant until it closed. Now he fishes, gardens, and does woodwork. Together we collect antiques. We have four daughters and seven grandchildren. The children like to visit and go fishing.

Betty's Shoepeg Salad

1 can shoepeg (white) corn
1 can petite peas
1 can French-style green
   beans
1 cup onions, chopped fine
1 cup celery, chopped fine
Small amount chopped
   pimento or red pepper
   for color

SYRUP
1 cup granulated sugar
⅔ cup vinegar
½ cup oil

Drain vegetables well. Boil the sugar, vinegar, and oil to make a syrup. Cool, then mix all ingredients thoroughly. Keeps well.

Maxine Thomas

I have lived a full and exciting life in Beardstown, where I was born and raised. I graduated from Beardstown High School during the Depression with no hope of going to college. I had worked at the Woolworth store on Saturdays during my senior year, so after graduation I was fortunate to be hired full-time to work behind the hardware counter.

Beardstown has always been a farming community that uses the railroads and Illinois River for loading grain. In World War II days, river traffic was heavy, with grain, coal, and oil barges. Beautiful excursion boats with dinner theater and dance bands would come down the river several times a year. It was on one of these excursion boats that I met my future husband, and a year later we were married.

Roy and I were blessed with two sons, and we purchased a home, a five-room bungalow on a large corner lot, in 1941 for $2,100. I am still living in the same house. My husband made enough money, employed at Schultz, Baujan Flour and Feed Mill, so that I did not have to work outside the home as so many mothers do today.

Our oldest son, Dick, who is married and has three children, still lives in Beardstown. Our youngest son, Ken, was on the staff of Chicago's Northwestern Memorial Hospital in 1986 when he passed away at the age of 33.

In 1960, when Dick started college, I started working at First National Bank, at age 40. This was an exciting time in our lives. I found myself fascinated by the business world, and I loved it. I started in the bookkeeping department and was promoted to teller, then loan officer, and finally assistant cashier. During this period, I joined the Business and Professional Women's Club, of which I was president for two years.

My husband and I had always been active in church and volunteer work, but we also found time to travel all over the United States, to Hawaii twice, and to the Caribbean Islands. We went to Europe in 1980 for our 40th anniversary. My husband died two months later.

BPW helped me through a very difficult time when I needed to know more about investing. The friendships I enjoyed in the Investment Club, and the education I received, has meant so very much.

My son Ken had been an individual investor and passed his investments on at his death to his nephew and nieces. They are learning about investing at a young age, along with their parents and grandma. Club member and good friend Lillian Ellis and I are still traveling, learning, earning, and enjoying life.

Maxine's Raw Apple Cake

1 cup sugar	2 beaten eggs
½ cup brown sugar	1 cup milk
1 tsp. baking powder	½ cup shortening
1 tsp. baking soda	1 tsp. vanilla
1 tsp. salt	2 cups apples (peeled and
1 tsp. cinnamon	diced)
2¼ cups all-purpose flour	1 cup chopped pecans

Combine all ingredients except apples and ½ cup pecans and mix well. Fold in the diced apples and mix well. Place in ungreased 9 × 13 pan. Sprinkle 2 tbsp. sugar and ½ cup chopped pecans over top. Bake 30 to 40 minutes in a 350 degree oven.

Buffy Tillitt-Pratt

I joined the club in 1987. I've owned my own real estate business, Buffy Tillitt & Associates, for 15 years. I am a director at a local bank, and am fascinated by earnings and financial potential.

Before joining the club, I tried investing in the stock market one time by purchasing stock in the drug company, Searle. I was always dieting, and when I first tasted Nutra-Sweet, I knew it was a good product, so I ran out and bought stock in the company that made it. I bought 50 shares by scrimping and saving, hoping to get in on the "ground floor" of this great invention. But it was taken off the exchange one and one-half years after I bought it. The company bought back my shares at a profit.

Since I usually arrive at meetings straight from work, I haven't had dinner and am starved. Then we start looking at our stock company's annual reports. There are the ones from Hershey's with beautiful color pictures of candy bars

and chocolate, and McDonalds with hamburgers and french fries. While I'm listening to their profit reports, I'm thinking about which of their products I can eat as soon as the meeting ends! Sometimes I can't go to the meetings because I am showing real estate in the evenings, but I like the instructional part of being a member. At every meeting there is something new to learn. I enjoy reading Forbes, Better Investing, *and* Value-Line *as much as browsing through any women's magazine about decorating or food.*

I have lived in this area all my life. My dad was the Ford dealer and the mayor of Beardstown, as well as a big inspiration to me in financial matters. My mother worked for my dad for over 40 years and never received her own paycheck. I think it is important for women to have their own money, to invest, to spend, even to lose. Whether they learn by their mistakes, their success, or by education in a club like ours, it is important that they have that opportunity to learn. My husband has a business also. He is a boat dealer. I help him with bookkeeping and other business matters, but we have separate checking accounts, and separate money, which is vital to our relationship.

I had my first child, Tillitt James Pratt, when I was 40. I bring my son to work with me. There are four people in my office, so between us we can take care of him. It's a beautiful plan. T. J. Pratt is my most important asset, even though he doesn't show up on the asset side of my financial statement. The fellowship and comradeship of the women in the club are the true assets of the Beardstown Business and Professional Women's Investment Club. Profits and education may be our claim to fame, but friendship helps hold the club together.

Buffy's Busy Woman's Dream

1 lb. uncooked ground turkey 1 can cream of chicken soup
1 can mixed vegetables

Stir all ingredients together and spoon into casserole dish. Top with Tater Tots. Bake at 375 degrees for 1 hour. (The only challenge is finding a free hour in which to bake it.)

Five Beardstown Ladies are active in NAIC's *Heart of Illinois Regional Investment Council. Maxine Thomas is associate director and historian; Helen Kramer is secretary; Betty Sinnock is past president and Co-Fair Chairman; Shirley Gross is parliamentarian; and Lillian Ellis is a member of the Audit Committee.*

21. Another Kind of Reward . . . Helping Others

We don't think it's an overstatement that you're never too old to learn. That's why education has always been the keystone of our efforts, and is a continuing part of what the club is all about. When we started out, we wanted to learn about the stock market so we could feel good about investing our own money. Today they call that "empowerment," or being "self-actualized" . . . but for us it seemed like common sense to be able to handle our own finances. We are always trying to learn more and, frankly, if the club stopped making money tomorrow—which we hope it doesn't—we would be able to look back with satisfaction on the educational efforts of our little group. Learning gives you a great feeling of accomplishment and it's something we recommend to everyone who reads this book, whether young or old, male or female, in a group or on your own. Study the market in order to learn and you will have a good profit no matter how your dollar investments fare. Reinvest that profit by helping others to learn and you will be rewarded over and over again.

One of the ways in which we try to help others is through our efforts with the NAIC, especially the Heart of Illinois Council. There's hardly a week that goes by when one of our members isn't traveling somewhere in the state to give a seminar or meet with a new club. And, of course, we encourage the new groups to make education a part of what they do too. These educational "investments" have been growing substantially over the last ten years and we now have a fine network of friends and fellow investors all across the state with whom we share experiences and advice. We also make presentations to high school classes, civic groups, and others who are interested in hearing the story of The Beardstown Ladies. Senior citizens, teenagers, young marrieds, and people from every walk of life seem to want to know how we accomplished our goals, and we're always ready to share our recipe for success.

Helping others is also why we first agreed to appear on television when a producer from *CBS This Morning* gave Betty a call in 1991. It seems they were interested in doing a story on investment clubs in the Midwest and had called the NAIC in Royal Oak, Michigan, for a suggestion. When they mentioned that our club had been named an All-Star Club for four consecutive years, they decided to use us as an example. The first time the big TV remote truck came to Beardstown it caused quite a stir! We had to arrive at the town square early in the morning and went on nationwide live. Not all of us could hear the questions, but Betty and Shirley were able to talk a little about the advantages of being in a club. In our minds, this was well worth the effort because it would encourage others to get involved in investing.

It must have worked, because a few months later CBS sent financial editor John Stehr back to town for another appearance. This time we met in the historic Park House Hotel and were interviewed in person by John and from New York by Paula Zahn (Harry was on vacation). Before we knew it, we were getting calls and letters from all around the country, from people trying to find out more about us. Some of them came simply addressed to "The Beardstown Ladies, Beardstown, Illinois." Some people just wanted a "get-rich-quick" stock tip, but most were sincere about learning. We tried to answer each of the letters with information and encouragement, as much as time allowed.

It seems like one good thing always leads to another, and it was true in this case too. Keith Colter, a filmmaker from Chicago, saw an article about our being on TV in the Springfield, Illinois, paper (his hometown). He came to Beardstown, attended one of our meetings, and asked us if we'd like to be featured in an educational video about investment clubs. After some discussion, the club agreed that this would be a good way to help others learn about investing. The club voted to go ahead with the project, provided that we only had to contribute our time and expertise and not any money. This was agreeable to Keith and his company, Central Picture, and before we knew it a film crew was following us around town, going to meetings and interviewing all of our members. The project seemed to grow and grow and before long what had started out as a 20-minute educational video was an hour-long program on our club entitled "Cookin' Up Profits on Wall Street." The video was finished at the end of 1992. Then CBS decided to come back to Beardstown for a third story on our group. It looked like we were on the way to getting some real publicity!

As Central Picture began marketing our videotape

around the country, sending out dozens of press packets and telling the story of The Beardstown Ladies to anyone who would listen, we found out just how interested people were in our story. Our phones began to ring off the hook as reporters and journalists from across the country wanted to hear how we had beaten the market. We began doing dozens of interviews in person and over the telephone with articles appearing in *Bottomline, Kiplinger's Personal Finance, Modern Maturity, Successful Retirement, Money, Chicago* magazine, and many, many others. Shirley still keeps up our scrapbook and clips every article she can find, but there were literally dozens of articles in newspapers and newletters in 1993.

Perhaps one of the most satisfying experiences we had that year was when "Cookin' Up Profits on Wall Street" was awarded a prestigious National Media Owl Award by the Retirement Research Foundation for its positive portrayal in the media of senior citizens. The awards were presented in Chicago, and a number of us made the trip. Gene Siskel and Ann Landers were the co-hosts and we got to meet them both. Gene couldn't help kidding us through the entire program about giving him a stock tip, and finally he stopped the ceremony and had the house lights brought up. He said he wasn't going to finish the show until we told him what our secret was! Betty stood up and told him about our latest purchase . . . Rubbermaid. After Gene's antics, half the audience probably went home and the next morning tried to buy Rubbermaid.

After that, things seemed to get even more hectic. As representatives of the club, Betty and Maxine were invited to appear on *The Home Show* with Gary Collins, and again with John Tesh and Leeza Gibbons on their talk show, *John and Leeza's Hollywood*. Each time they went to Los Angeles they got to stay in a nice hotel and ride in a limousine, but had hardly any time at all for sightseeing. We were getting more and more requests for information and could barely get business done at our meetings because so many guests and reporters were there. Finally, we had to restrict our visitors to just three meetings a year, and began to turn down personal appearances. We felt bad that we couldn't meet with everyone who wrote or called, but we realized that we weren't sticking to one of our original guidelines—to invest, learn, and *have fun.* If our meetings weren't fun anymore, we'd have to find new ways to reach people. That's one of the reasons we agreed to write this book.

Education is still one of the greatest goals of our club, and we have certainly continued to learn as we appeared on TV, in video, and now as writers. By trying to help others accomplish their goals, we're still accomplishing many of our own. In 1993, Betty Sinnock was named The Thomas O'Hara Award Winner by the NAIC at the national convention in Portland, Oregon. This public-service award is given by the NAIC to the member who does the most to promote the principles of NAIC and to help educate others. It is a very important award, and we are all very proud of Betty. With her election to the National Board of Directors of the NAIC this year, she is constantly traveling, attending conferences, leading seminars, and spreading the word about do-it-yourself investing. We feel that she carries the spirit of our little club with her everywhere she goes.

As our book goes to press, we are looking forward to many more years of successful investing together. Recently, we took in a new member, Carol McCombs. As we watch Carol learn and grow in her understanding of the ways of Wall Street, we can think proudly of the thousands of others who might have read about us or seen us on TV and decided to try to manage at least a portion of their own finances. We truly hope that our legacy will not be measured so much in dollars but in the knowledge and self-confidence that, hopefully, people will pass on to their friends, their children, and to others who have learned about investing "The Beardstown Ladies way."

> **"One thing we learned in farming is that you never rely on one source. The more sources you have, the more educated your decisions."**
>
> **—CARNELL KORSMEYER**

Resources We Recommend

We can't possibly list all of the valuable resources available to investors. Instead, the following is a list of those organizations and references that have been most useful to our club.

Organizations

National Association of Investors Corporation
711 W. Thirteen-Mile Road
Madison Heights, MI 48071
(810/583-6242)

International Association for Financial Planning
Two Concourse Parkway, Suite 800
Atlanta, GA 30328
(404/395-1605)

Books

Peter Lynch, with John Rothchild. *One Up on Wall Street.* New York: Simon & Schuster, 1989.

————. *Beating the Street.* New York: Simon & Schuster, 1993.

John Train. *The Midas Touch, The Strategies That Have Made Warren Buffett "America's Pre-eminent Investor."* New York: Harper & Row, 1987.

Jane Bryant Quinn. *Making the Most of Your Money.* New York: Simon & Schuster, 1991.

Terry Savage. *Terry Savage Talks Money: The Common Sense Guide to Money Matters.* New York: Harper Perennial, 1991.

Thomas E. O'Hara and Helen J. McLane. *Taking Control of Your Financial Future.* Burr Ridge, IL: Richard D. Irwin Inc., 1995.

Helen McLane. *NAIC's Investors Manual.* NAIC. 15th edition, 1992. (Available from NAIC, address above.)

Periodicals

Value Line Investment Survey
220 East 42nd Street
New York, NY 10017
(212/907-1500)
(See the discount offer at the end of this book.)

Standard & Poor's Stock Reports
25 Broadway
New York, NY 10004
(212/208-8000)

Moody's Handbook of Common Stocks
Moody's Investor's Service, Inc.
99 Church Street
New York, NY 10007
(212/553-0300)

BusinessWeek
McGraw-Hill, Inc.
1221 Avenue of the Americas
New York, NY 10020
(212/512-2000)

Fortune
Time, Inc.
Time and Life Building
Rockefeller Center
New York, NY 10020
(212/522-1212)

Forbes
60 Fifth Avenue
New York, NY 10011
(212/620-2200)

The Wall Street Journal
200 Liberty
New York, NY
(212/416-2000)

Kiplinger's Personal Finance Magazine
1729 H St. N.W.
Washington, DC 20006
(202/887-6400)

Video

To order the Ladies' award-winning video, "Cookin' Up Profits on Wall Street," call 1-800-359-EARN. (Or use the convenient coupon at the end of this book.)

Glossary

Acid test ratio (also known as the quick ratio): The value of a company's marketable securities, cash, and accounts receivable divided by its total current liabilities. Determines whether a company can quickly raise enough cash to cover its debts. A ratio of at least 1:1 is a standard benchmark.

Annual report: Yearly write-up of a public corporation's business, including comprehensive financial statements. Mailed to shareholders; available to the public on request.

Asset: Something of value to a company or individual. Company assets include machinery, plants, and accounts receivable. Individual assets include homes, savings accounts, securities, collectibles, and insurance policies.

Balance sheet: A financial statement that gives a snapshot of a company's assets, liabilities, and capital on a specific date.

Beta: A number that compares the volatility (movement) of a stock's price relative to that of the total market. A beta of 1 means that a stock price moves up and down at the same rate as the market as a whole. A beta of 2 means that when the market drops or rises 10%, the stock price is likely to move double that, or 20%. A beta of .5 means that if the market rises 10%, the stock will likely rise only 5%.

Book value per share: Net worth divided by the number of shares outstanding. This number tells you what each share would be worth if the company was suddenly liquidated, based on balance sheet figures.

Broker: An individual who arranges for a transfer in the ownership of security between a buyer and seller. Brokers charge a fee for this service.

Capital gain: The profit from the sale of a capital asset, such as securities or a home.

Capital gains tax: Tax levied on the difference between the cost of a capital asset and the sale price. Capital gains are taxed at a maximum rate of 28%.

Capital loss: The loss incurred when a capital asset is sold for less than it was purchased for.

Cash flow: The net income of a company plus any non-cash deductions from income, such as depreciation. A measure of a company's ability to cover expenses and pay dividends.

Cash flow statement: A report of a company's cash flow over a period of time, which gives a good indication of the firm's ability to pay debt.

Certificates of deposit (CDs): A bank-issued investment that pays a specified amount of interest depending on the amount of money invested and the length of time it is deposited in the bank, usually between three months and three years. Interest is earned at maturity.

Common stock: A share of stock represents a fractional ownership of a corporation. Shareholders elect the board of directors, thereby indirectly controlling the management of the company. If a company dissolves, common stockholders have last claim on assets after bondholders, other creditors, and preferred stockholders.

Convert to cash: Sell.

Corporation: An organization created by law. Its share-holders have limited liability.

Current assets: Company assets which may be converted into cash within a year. They are listed in the balance sheet in the order of the ease with which they can be converted to cash: cash; government securities; accounts receivable; and inventories.

Current liabilities: Liabilities that must be paid off within a year.

Current ratio: Current assets divided by current liabilities.

Depreciation: Deduction allowed to account for the cost of an asset that will wear out over a period of time.

Diversify: Spread risk by investing in a wide variety of stocks, industries, and/or types of securities.

Dividend: Portion of retained earnings paid to stockhold-ers, either in cash or stock.

Dollar cost averaging: Investing a constant amount in a security at regular intervals, regardless of fluctuations in mar-ket price. Over time, this investment method will result in sav-ings because more shares will be bought when the price dips and fewer shares will be bought when the price rises. The re-sult: the average cost per share to the investor will be lower than the average cost of the security during that period.

Dow Jones Industrial Average: The average price of 30 leading industrial stocks traded on the New York Stock Exchange.

Earnings per share: Divide net income, after subtracting preferred dividends, by the number of shares of common stock.

Earnings predictability: A *Value Line* rating that measures the degree to which a company's earnings are predictable based on past performance. Scale: 100 (most predictable) to 5 (least predictable). NMF is used to denote no prediction.

Equity: Same as *net worth*. The difference between assets and liabilities.

Financial strength: A *Value Line* rating based on its analysts' examination of a company's financial condition. Scale: A^{++} (strongest) to C (weakest).

Fixed assets: Assets, such as property, plant, and equipment, that the company does not expect to convert into cash within a year.

Income statement: A chart of a company's profitability over time; part of an annual report.

Industry rank: A company's rating within its industry based on its timeliness ranking by *Value Line*.

Liabilities: The claims of creditors.

Long-term debt: Debt, such as bonds, secured by company property.

NAIC: National Association of Investors Corporation, a nonprofit organization that provides educational materials and programs to individual investors and investment clubs.

Net income: Profit after taxes.

Net sales: Amount of money collected for goods and services sold minus returns and allowances.

Net worth: All assets minus all liabilities.

Odd lot: Less than 100 shares of stock purchased at one time.

Operating costs and expenses: Expenses including the cost of goods sold, marketing, administration, and research and development.

Operating income: Net sales minus operating costs and expenses.

Paper loss or **Paper profit**: A loss or profit that you would make *if* you sold your stock at a particular price, so called because these gains and losses are nothing more than calculations made on a piece of a paper. They do not become "real" until the security is actually sold.

Portfolio: The securities held by an individual investor, institutional investor, or investment club.

Preferred stock: Stock with claims to dividends and assets that take precedence over those of common stock.

Price-earnings ratio: Price of a share of stock divided by the company's earnings per share.

Price growth persistence: A *Value Line* rating that measures a stock's price performance compared to predictions based on past performance. Scale: 100 (most persistent) to 5 (least). NMF is used for no prediction available.

Private corporation: A privately held corporation that does not offer stock for sale to the public. Few reporting requirements.

Public corporation: A corporation that offers ownership through stock to the public. Required by law to disclose specific information about its financial condition and operations.

Revenues: Sales.

Safety: A ranking, made by *Value Line*, that measures the volatility of a stock's price. Scale: 1 (least volatile) to 5 (most volatile).

Sales per employee: Net sales divided by number of employees.

Securities: Investment instruments, including stocks and bonds.

Securities and Exchange Commission (SEC): Federal agency that regulates the sale of securities.

Shareholders' equity: The value of preferred and common stock.

Stock price stability: A rating by *Value Line* designed to measure a stock's volatility in relation to the market. Scale: 100 (most stable) to 5 (least stable). NMF is used when there is no degree of measure.

Stock Selection Guide: An NAIC form designed to assist investors evaluate stocks.

Stock split: When a company issues a number of shares for each share of stock outstanding. Example: a 3-for-2 split means shareholders receive three shares for every two they own; so a shareholder who owns 10 shares trading at $3 a share before a 3-for-2 split will own 15 shares trading at $2 a share after the split. The purpose is to broaden ownership and make the stock price more attractive.

Stockholder: Synonymous with shareholder.

Timeliness: A ranking, made by *Value Line*, that measures a stock's predicted price performance over the next year. Scale: 1 (most timely) to 5 (least timely).

Total assets: Current assets plus net property, plant, and equipment.

Total liabilities: Current liabilities plus long-term debt.

Unit value system: An investment club accounting method.

Upside-down ratio: A measurement of risk on NAIC forms. Divide the projected high price of a stock by its projected low.

Yield: The annual dividend per share divided by price of the stock.

Index

Entries in *italics* refer to tables and illustrations.

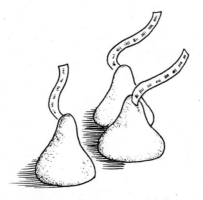

The Beardstown Ladies are 16 women who are members of an investment club that was established more than 10 years ago. They all live in or near Beardstown, Illinois, and still meet on the first Thursday of every month.

Leslie Whitaker, formerly a reporter for *Time* magazine, is a freelance writer based in Oak Park, Illinois.

Seth Godin Productions is a team of writers and editors that creates books in Dobbs Ferry, New York. To date, they have more than 75 books in print, ranging from books on business to computers to education.

THE BEARDSTOWN LADIES

NOW MEET THE LADIES IN THEIR OWN VIDEO!

Shot on location in Beardstown, Illinois this one hour video gives you the flavor and spirit of the Ladies "up close and personal." The Beardstown Ladies' award-winning videotape, *Cookin' Up Profits on Wall Street*, tells you everything you need to know to create your own common-sense financial plan, organize and run your own investment club, and look for companies using the same fundamentals the Ladies use. It includes interviews with all of the members of the club as well as point by point explanations of key areas. Great for individual investors or investment clubs, old or new!

Mature Media
1994
NATIONAL AWARDS
WINNER

Gold Medal Winner
National Mature Marketing Award

Winner,
National Media Owl Award

"Of the financial videos . . . the most entertaining."—*MONEY* **magazine**

"A superb guide for potential investment club organizers . . . as well as individual investors."—*Booklist*

To order your own copy at $10.00 off the regular price of $29.95, call

1-800-359-3276

MasterCard, Visa, or Discover accepted. Ask for offer #27. Or use the coupon below for check or money order.

NAME _____

ADDRESS _____

CITY _____ STATE _____ ZIP _____

YES! Please rush me ____ VHS copies of *Cookin' Up Profits on Wall Street* at $19.95 plus $3.25 shipping and handling each. (Illinois residents please add sales tax at 6.25%)

I have enclosed my check or money order for _____.
Mail to: Central Picture, 2222 W. Diversey #310, Chicago, IL 60647.
Please allow 4–6 weeks for delivery.

The Value Line Investment Survey®
220 East 42nd Street, New York, NY 10017-5891

A Special offer from Value Line

Receive a TRIAL subscription to
The Value Line Investment Survey

for $~~$65~~ $45

The most widely used investment publication, hailed as an invaluable information resource by

The Beardstown Ladies

is yours at the special price indicated, when you purchase this book describing the Beardstown Ladies' investment methods.

As a new Value Line subscriber, you receive the following:

- Full "Investor's Reference Library" containing the most recent Value Line reports on all 1,700 companies and 98 industries.

- Your own copy of "How to Invest in Common Stocks," our guide to using **The Value Line Investment Survey.**

- Ten full weeks of current editions, each updating some 130 company reports and seven industry reviews, with new Timeliness™ and Safety Ranks and current data on all 1,700 stocks.

To order, indicate on a card or in a letter your preferred option, with your name, mailing address, and telephone number (with the source code indicated below), and send this information to us, with your payment (check or current credit-card information: VISA, MasterCard or American Express), at the address indicated above.

To qualify for this special offer, you MUST include the following source code: NTBL

- ❑ 10-week trial of Value Line for $45 — (available only once every three years to any household; not available to current subscribers)

- ❑ One year (52 issues) of Value Line for $465 — (regular price: $525)

Money-Back Guarantee

If you are not satisfied, for any reason, you may return the materials within 30 days for a full refund of the subscription fee paid. Your subscription to Value Line may be tax-deductible. Consult your tax advisor.
